Gloria ✐ W9-BVV-671

HARVEST

HARVEST

CHUCK SMITH
AND TAL BROOKE

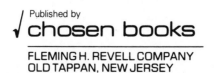
Published by
chosen books

FLEMING H. REVELL COMPANY
OLD TAPPAN, NEW JERSEY

Library of Congress Cataloging in Publication Data

Smith, Chuck, 1927 June 25–
  Harvest.

  "Chosen books."
  1. Calvary Chapel (Costa Mesa, Calif.)—History.
2. Costa Mesa (Calif.)—Church history.   I. Brooke,
Tal.   II. Title.
BX9999.C653S65   1987   289.9   87-26544
ISBN 0-8007-9114-2
All rights reserved. No part of this publication may be reproduced, stored
in a retrieval system, or transmitted in any form or by any means without
the prior permission of the publisher.

A Chosen Book
Copyright © 1987 by Chuck Smith
Chosen Books are published by
Fleming H. Revell Company
Old Tappan, New Jersey
Printed in the United States of America

Contents

Foreword

One of the constant frustrations that we as Christians face is that of seeking to know the unknowable. We would like to figure out God's ways. Yet God Himself has said, "My ways are not your ways; My ways are beyond your finding out."

When God desired to bring the nation Israel to the apex of its power, He chose an unlikely person to lead them to this place of glory as their king. From the house of Jesse, in the city of Bethlehem, He anointed the youngest son, David, whose only qualifications were that he was a shepherd who loved God and that he reflected on His greatness as it was revealed to him in nature.

When God wanted to raise up a mighty army for David to lead against Israel's foes, He gathered those who were distressed, in debt, and discontented. These unlikely soldiers became David's mighty men and through them, God defeated all of their enemies.

When Jesus wanted to turn the world upside-down, and bring the message of God's love to all mankind, He chose unlikely candidates. Of the twelve, most were fishermen and one was a hated publican. These are certainly not the choices we would have made for the task.

When God wanted to make an impact on our society, He again chose the foolish things, as far as the world is concerned, to confound the wise; He chose the weak things to confound the mighty.

For instance, in raising up pastors to shepherd some

churches with thousands of members, God did not nec-
essarily look for Phi Beta Kappas from Yale or Harvard; He
did not look for *magna cum laude* graduates who then went
on to become Ph.D's. Instead, in our case, God chose a
Mexican street fighter who had dropped out of high
school, a hippie who had gone insane on drugs, a drug
dealer who was into sorcery, and a motorcycle gang
member, for the task of building His churches in the
Calvary Chapel movement. These are just a few of the
unlikely leaders God has used in our ministries to turn
worn traditions upside-down.

In these pages, you are going to read the incredible,
indeed, almost unbelievable accounts of men with varied,
wild, and even Satanic backgrounds, who were touched by
the grace of God, and who are now touching thousands of
others with the same grace. As you read, you will no doubt
wonder how these men, who for the most part had no
formal education for the ministry, were able to go out and
build churches ranging in size from several thousand to ten
thousand members.

What are the common factors? What are the things they
learned that enabled them to experience such phenomenal
success in their ministries? Their stories are only a sam-
pling of the scores of others that we have watched come
into our church over the years, men who have been
transformed by the power of the Spirit of God, and are
now pastoring in the several hundred churches that have
grown out of our fellowship.

We are convinced that the concepts that the Lord has
taught us in forty years of ministry are transferable to
others. And if followed, they can help build strong
churches all over the country.

In the book of Acts, we read that at the birth of the

Church 3,000 souls were added to the number of believers the very first day. Then the Lord continued to add daily such as should be saved. We are convinced that when the Church becomes what God intended it to be, God will do through the Church what He has always desired to do: Through the power of His grace He will bring in a harvest of souls that can only humble our loftiest plans. Indeed, His ways are not always our ways. If we will only but hear His voice.

Chuck Smith
Calvary Chapel of Costa Mesa

Preface

I blotted my forehead and opened recent copies of *Look*, *Time*, and *Newsweek* magazines. Full-page photographs held me spellbound.

Sweat dripped down my arms as I stood holding the magazines in a hot crowded South Indian bazaar. I was at a roadside stand near the Bangalore bus station in Mysore State. I was returning to the headquarters of Sai Baba, the biggest guru in India. At the time, I was a member of his inner circle.

A human form almost jumped out of one picture: a glistening body was plunging up from the Pacific Ocean, standing, arms outstretched toward the blue heavens above. It was a microsecond frozen in time. Particles of ocean spray hung crystallized in space. Water, frozen like glass, cascaded down his torso. A million droplets of water beaded his skin like jewels. His face seemed to hold an ocean of joyous ecstasy. Blissful relief turned his countenance into a smiling cathedral of hope.

He was a vintage California hippie: tanned with long golden hair that clung to a lean, muscular chest. The road map of this fellow's past could still be seen in his veins and face: from shooting and popping drugs in Haight Ashbury to eating sun-ripened fruit and thumbing along Route 1 between San Francisco and L.A. But the face coming out of the ocean indicated that the journey had come to a joyous and unexpected end. No more striving. No more hell. Infinite peace rested on this fortunate soul.

The young man in the picture had just been baptized in a cove at Corona Del Mar Beach. He had made his immense journey from Golden Gate to eternity and was one of nine hundred people baptized that day by Calvary Chapel. The Jesus Movement was going full-gear on the California coast.

The main figure performing the baptisms in the other pictures was Chuck Smith, the man behind the Calvary Chapel phenomenon that was sweeping the West Coast and other parts of America. For months, they had been baptizing an average of nine hundred youths a month. It was a phenomenon that was bewildering the secular pundits, from Marcuse to Leary.

The pictures indicated that the crowd standing in the Pacific and along the rock bluff had abandoned the dreams of the counterculture to become Christians, casting their lives and burdens on Jesus Christ. They had abandoned the whole parcel of wild pleasures and freedoms—drugs, communal living, rejection of social norms, free sex, and all of the Eastern spiritualities that tagged along with this radical life experiment—in order to adopt Christianity, of all things. To me in India, the pictures suggested a serious setback. The old world biblical view, with its black and white paradigms, was getting a new foothold. Why? Sooner than I dared think I would know the answer to that question.

For two years, I had been in India following the "consciousness expansion" regimen of a self-proclaimed God-man, who told me that I was destined for enlightenment. I was riding the crest of a mystical wave that would help bring the New Age movement to America in the coming ten years. It was a real-life drama that had all the intrigue of an adventure movie. But the magazine picture before me was an affront to all that I believed; it signaled opposition to the gathering momentum of our "new consciousness."

As I focused on the picture, I reflected on the enormous difficulty of my own spiritual path toward "godhood." As of late I had been feeling the road-weariness and discouragement that can come from the Eastern spiritual path. And, recently, some spiritual "tests" impeded my path—in the form of two Christian missionaries. Their love was disquieting. They literally radiated a wholesome goodness; and in even the most adverse of circumstances, they rejoiced. They had a hidden spring of love and hope that never seemed to yield to outward circumstance. But as for me, being "advanced" as I was, I often found myself cursing all the things that sullied my trail to eternal perfection.

Look magazine's February 1971 cover story, and the articles in the other magazines, captured a surprising social phenomenon. The '60s era was speeding down a number of diverse social highways as it was coming to a close. The counterculture was being portrayed in the picture—but there was a surprise fork in the road. California's radical hippie culture, embodied by the rejoicing nomad in the picture, was suddenly caught in a strange juxtaposition. A photograph of a flower child dripping in the Pacific surf was no surprise. But the reason for his being there was!

Within a year of that quiet moment at the Indian roadside stand, I, like the fellow pictured in the magazine, would be submerged in a lake near Charlottesville, Virginia, and come out with the same smile of relief and joy. For the first time in my life I would know real hope.

Little did I know at the time that, not only would I

abandon my guru, but I would become a Christian. And in time I would even end up working with the same central figure in the photographs, Chuck Smith himself. The article was like God's quiet signal to my soul saying, "You think you are on the path to truth but you have been seduced into believing the most subtle lie in the world. Do you see that figure standing in the waves? That is My servant Chuck Smith. Someday, by My timetable, you will link up with him in the fellowship of ministry."

But that was in the future. At the time I only knew that, along with most of my generation, I had rejected the Christian alternative.

How did it happen? How did we get off the track in the first place? In some ways I was a model case.

A GENERATION IN CHAOS

I grew up in an atheistic home; we never went to church. Besides that, I had an early introduction into the occult. While my father was a diplomat in London—I was ten years old—he took me up on a dare one evening and brought home a Ouija board with which to experiment. As a convinced materialist, as far as he was concerned all I was doing was engaging in a harmless superstition.

By the time I was an undergraduate at the University of Virginia, I was deeply into mysticism. The door blew open for me when I took a massive dose of Sandoz LSD in the Virginia countryside. It was one of those warm spring evenings when the meadows seemed like a vast armchair. After the celestial powers had finished talking to me and I was certain that I had been given a glimpse of eternity, no one could keep me away from the Upanishads and other Indian holy books. I had a gut-directed sense that one day I would go to India in search of an enlightened master.

But let me make another confession. One of the key reasons I dismissed Christianity and turned to Eastern thought was because of what I saw in the churches I tried attending. The love that is so enthrallingly reported in the New Testament Church wasn't very evident in those modern churches. In fact its absence was louder than thunder. A small-minded judgmentalism often accompanied a chilly aloofness. And I felt that even the more conservative churches were not willing to share what they had with anyone who did not meet their particular standards.

To an outsider, there is nothing more sordid than when the grace and beauty of God have departed from a church, for what remains is the outward display of religion without the inner heart and soul. Thus, they became irrelevant in my eyes.

But it was not all the fault of closed-minded churches: My generation fell into its own trap. The wild permissiveness of the counterculture thought itself more honest in its own eyes than the "judgmental hypocrisy" it saw in the Church. We wrote off the Church prematurely. So, like my counterparts, I looked upon the overtures of the Church with acute suspicion. For instance, I submitted the two missionaries in India, whom I mentioned earlier, to ruthless scrutiny. And what shone out of these two faithful souls was the unhindered grace of God. I reached the end of my road when I encountered the genuine article of God's grace. The caricature of the Church could no longer be an excuse for me. Indeed, during some of my drier years as a Christian, I too could be accused of the very things for which I once vehemently attacked the Church. I too was often intolerant, judgmental, and unloving.

To say the least, it takes a powerful ministry to reach a group as alienated and hostile to the Church in general as the youth of the '60s and '70s. So when these people, from all sorts of backgrounds, encountered the ministry of Calvary Chapel, whatever it was that they saw, it was enough to disarm them and turn them around.

When I finally strolled into the airy sanctuary of Calvary Chapel of Costa Mesa ten years after my conversion, what I felt was like a refreshing breeze. I felt an abundant flow of love the moment I walked through the door. There was not even a fleeting hint of judgmentalism here. Rather, I felt a terrific sense of belonging. I noticed something else about the man in the pulpit. I had long wondered about that promise God gave His people: that out of them would flow rivers of living water. Without any question, I saw this happen with Chuck Smith as he spoke. This to me signaled God's seal on the work. Chuck Smith lost himself in God's abundance as he pointed to God and never to himself.

When I met Chuck Smith after the service, it was like meeting an old friend. Many people thronged in line to meet him; attendance of the three Sunday morning services numbered over four thousand apiece. When my turn in line came to meet Chuck Smith, I am not sure I have ever met anyone more gracious, open, and loving. I could see why God used this humble soul to reach an entire generation. I also knew that his ministry was not just limited to reaching that one generation.

Calvary Chapel started from a humble base. But it was

willing to become relevant to a dying generation. The result is perhaps the greatest harvest of souls by a single church in American history. There are some exciting lessons in this for all of us. And it is these lessons that this book hopes to pursue.

Tal Brooke

HARVEST

Top row (*from left*): Jon Courson, Mike MacIntosh, **bottom row:** Steve Mays, Jeff Johnson, Greg Laurie, Don McClure, Raul Ries, Skip Heitzig, Chuck Smith, Tal Brooke

1

Calvary Chapel Enters History

As I describe to you the explosion of church growth that happened to us across the Calvary Chapel ministries, starting with my Costa Mesa church, I speak as a spectator. If there is any boasting, it is the Lord's. Once you glimpse this perspective, then when I describe to you my difficult years, my desert years, you will know why I stand in awe at what God has done. And you will celebrate with me over the awesome symmetry of God's design. It leaves us all gaping spectators.

Those pictures in *Look, Life, Time,* and *Newsweek* magazines of our massive Calvary Chapel baptisms in the Pacific Ocean make them resemble a human harvest field. Literally thousands of people can be seen crowding the shores waiting to be baptized. These magazines make it evident that this is a colossal phenomenon as far as churches go. Professors such as Peter Wagner at Fuller and Ron Enroth at Westmont state in their books that there may be nothing like it in American history.

At one point it was estimated that in a two-year period in the mid-'70s, Calvary Chapel of Costa Mesa had performed well over eight thousand baptisms. During that same period, we were instrumental in 20,000 conversions to the Christian faith. Our decadal growth rate, according to church growth professors, was virtually at the remarkable ten thousand percent level.

Perhaps more staggering still is that when we first came to Calvary Chapel church in Costa Mesa in 1965, we had twenty-five people our first Sunday morning.

Now put this in perspective. Not only has that church of twenty-five members established more than three hundred affiliate Calvary Chapels across the United States, but that one fellowship in Costa Mesa has grown until the number of people who consider it their home church is more than thirty-five thousand! It is currently listed as number eighteen among the twenty largest churches in the entire world. John Vaughan, in *The World's Twenty Largest Churches*, devotes an entire chapter to the remarkable phenomenon of Calvary Chapel.

I have heard critics try to dismiss the impact of Calvary Chapel by calling it production line religion. They have accused us of catering to what people want to hear by diluting the message to appeal to the masses. Some critics, apparently, have decided what God can and cannot do—and He cannot do "the impossible."

Other critics, who belong to churches that have not grown in years, which was exactly my situation for well over a decade, often adopt a stance of spiritual elitism. To them, smallness proves spirituality, faithfulness, or unwillingness to compromise. Perhaps they feel that "quantity" diminishes the "quality" of spirituality.

Christ talked about the man who buried his talents and wound up with nothing, because even what he had was taken away. But He also spoke about the servant who magnified his talents a thousandfold. So to say, as the critics might, that Christ limits the size and impact of a ministry is unfounded. The explosive force of a ministry can well be a sign that God is genuinely at work. Who can forget the day of Pentecost when three thousand turned to Christ on the streets of Jerusalem? "And the Lord added to their number daily those who were being saved" (Acts 2:47).

Just as the Jews soon discovered that they were not to keep the Good News among themselves, but were to include the "despised" Gentiles, so there was an interesting shifting of gears at Calvary Chapel. The Good News was shared by that faithful fellowship of twenty-five members, who represented mainline America, with the youth from the counterculture. This reaching out took a miracle of love and acceptance. But, you know, as each group accepted the other, *both* sides grew in number. There was a vital sense of God stepping into the picture and as lives changed before our eyes, the sense of being in the middle of a miracle kept feeding itself like a bonfire. When some hopeless outcast, who has been addicted to heroin, throws away the needle and goes on the beach to convert three people to Christ in an afternoon, it's a pretty strong boost to your faith.

Another remarkable pattern kept repeating: As soon as we moved into a new building, our fellowship was already too big for the facilities. We seemed to grow like a Chinese checker jumping across the board. In two years we moved from our original building, one of the first church buildings in Costa Mesa, to a rented Lutheran church building overhanging the Pacific. Soon thereafter we decided to do the unpredictable at the time and move the church to a school that we had bought. The building did not match up to code so we tore it down and built another, hippies and straights working and smiling side by side. Sometimes cars on the highway would slow down and gawk at us.

I had always felt that the ideal church size was about 275 and so we built accordingly. But by the time the sanctuary of 330 seats was completed in 1969, we were already forced to go to two services, and eventually had to use the outside courtyard for 500 more seats. This was all fine in good weather.

By 1971, however, the large crowds and the winter rains forced us to move again. We bought a ten-acre tract of land on the Costa Mesa/Santa Ana border. Orange County was quickly changing and the once-famous orange orchards were making way for the exploding population of Los Angeles, as communities moved south. Soon after buying the land, we again did the unpredictable and erected a giant circus tent that could seat 1,600 at a stretch. This was soon enlarged to hold 2,000 seats. Meanwhile we began building an enormous sanctuary adjacent to it.

This was all amazing to me—and a bit frightening. I would sit at the signal across the street looking at the bare lot that we had obligated ourselves to purchase, and start to panic. It would take a tremendous amount of money to develop the property. Was I being foolish to obligate these people to that kind of a project? Why not be satisfied where you are? I would think. The bills are all paid. You've got money in the bank. This is going to take such a great outlay. But then, one time as I sat there, the Lord spoke to my heart: *Whose church is it?* I replied out loud, "It's Your church, Lord." *Then why are you worried about bankruptcy?*

It was a relief. A sense of frantic worry just rolled off me. The finances were not my responsibility. They were His. This was an extremely important lesson for me to learn. It is not my church. It's His church. And, besides, He was the one who had created the problem! He was the one who brought so many people in that we couldn't house them.

And He continued to bring people in. By the time Calvary Chapel fellowship had celebrated opening day in 1973 and moved into the vast new sanctuary of 2,200 seats, the building was already too small to contain the numbers turning out. We held three Sunday morning services and had more than 4,000 people at each one. Many had to sit on the carpeted floor; a large portion of floor space was left without pews so as to provide that option.

I had always felt it important to maintain a sense of intimate fellowship. For this reason, the building was designed with pillars and beams that break up the sanctuary into segments of two hundred to five hundred seats so that each person has the feeling of being in a congregation rather than in a large crowded auditorium. Even the carpeted floor offers an intimate sense of fellowship for those sitting there; it's not unlike sitting in a meadow. The front platform is simple and unornamented. The seats form a semi-circle, communicating that no one is more important than anyone else. It gives an air of fresh openness. Though vast, it avoids pretension.

Because the believers gather at four separate Sunday services, including the evening service, we are not able to meet at our church as one corporate group. But because we desire a corporate "celebration of the body," we meet bimonthly for fellowship rallies. But even at the Anaheim Convention Center, which seats ten thousand, we have to hold two rallies back-to-back since we cannot all fit at one time.

I keep abreast of all of the details of daily work at Calvary Chapel. I have also instructed my pastoral staff to tell me of any members who wish to see me personally. I make myself readily available and can be called through my secretary. I also make myself accessible to anyone who wants to see me after any of the Sunday morning services. I stand out front shaking hands, greeting people, and discussing anything they have on their hearts.

Calvary Chapel also ministers over the airwaves, and this must account for at least some of those who at times come long distances. A Nielsen survey indicated that our Sunday morning Calvary Chapel service is the most listened-to program in the area during the entire week. As of 1987, Calvary's outreach has included numerous radio programs, television broadcasts, and the production and distribution of tapes and records. The missions outreach is considerable. Calvary Chapel not only supports Wycliffe Bible Translators, Campus Crusade, Missionary Aviation Fellowship, and other groups, but we donate to Third World needs. At what I felt was a leading from the Lord, we built a radio station in San Salvador and gave it to the local pastors there. We also gave money to Open Doors to purchase the ship that, in tandem with a barge, delivered one million Bibles to mainland China. Our missions outreach budget exceeds the local expense budget by over 50%.

Calvary Chapel of Costa Mesa often averages two hundred conversions a week. For years new believers were put into the highly respected Navigators' fourteen-week home Bible study program. Since then, Calvary Chapel has developed its own course. As part of the course new believers can attend numerous evening Bible studies and classes taught during the week. I teach a study for young people on Monday nights, and an in-depth midweek evening Bible study. On other nights of the week, thousands attend the wide variety of Bible studies and fellowship groups.

Calvary Chapel never asks for money. It never asks its members for "faith pledges" or yearly pledges. And no appeal for funds of any kind is ever made over radio or television. To beg for money brings discredit to God, remains our unwritten rule. Financial integrity is central to this ministry. So much so that all of the salaries are considered low by usual standards. I limit myself and my family to a simple lifestyle while my ministry has enabled me to oversee millions of dollars. I want to be responsible to God for this money, for it is His money, not mine. I am merely a steward. This is important to me because I know that nonbelievers will be watching, and we are responsible for the way we witness to them.

I have always had problems with flashy Christian celebrities of the media who somehow wind up in palatial manor houses and otherwise glitter and gleam from God's money—funds sent in by innocent, trusting, or vulnerable followers in response to high-pressure sales tactics. A personality cult is dangerous, but perhaps fiscal extravagance and dishonesty is even more dangerous. The tragedy is that all that the public sees, and in the end believes, is this image of Christians. A friend of mine calls this "Operation Caricature." The public image of a Christian, from all this media vulgarity, creates a cynical distrust of all believers, and the assumption of insincerity, naïveté, or gullibility is applied to all of us *en masse*. Our faith is discredited.

I believe God has blessed us at Calvary Chapel with an exceptionally loving and open fellowship. Christ told us that the world will know we are His by our love for one another. This is our predominant emphasis. And how I pray that we Christians can show the world this standard. Certainly our Lord told us that our identification marks should involve love, but also purity and integrity of character of the highest order. Unfortunately, Christians are caricatured on the airwaves through those self-elected representatives who parade themselves before the public at large while the scandals of their private lives belie this image. Their lives are as risqué as TV soap operas, which brings mocking sneers of discredit from secular observers.

We have to show the world something better than that. Yet, sadly, that numberless host of unseen Christians across the centuries who have subsisted and denied themselves on and off the mission field, living in scrupulous integrity—the George Muellers, Hudson Taylors, and C. T. Studds—doesn't even gain a flicker from the media spotlight. These great lives pass by in quiet anonymity. God must help us correct these imbalances of our day and equip us to be the ambassadors of Christ we were called to be.

Let me say that in this Calvary Chapel phenomenon, I did not just walk into a church the size of an aircraft carrier and become an admiral. The church was not handed over to me, like an industrial magnate bequeathing an unworthy son some multinational enterprise. Instead, as I will share with you, I had to work from scratch and obey every new call that came from God, even when those calls seemed irrational. Behind it was blood, sweat, and tears as well as lessons.

One of the secrets of my preparation for this work, I am

convinced, was my desert years, those years of struggle. It was in this crucible, I believe, that God prepared my character for the coming work. God so often makes a mockery of outward circumstances. He repudiates the impossible if we will only but believe. And believe me, my situation looked absolutely impossible at times!

2

The Drought Before the Harvest

I am not your hireling. God has called me to be a shepherd of His Church. You had better find a replacement for me.

These thoughts marked the major turning point in my life. I felt God clearly speaking to my heart. And after more than seventeen years of drought, seventeen years of failure in the traditional forms of Christian ministry, I knew that this era of ministerial confinement was coming to an end. I had come to a place where I could no longer digest the stifling restrictive role I was required to play. Where was the room for the Holy Spirit to work creatively among us? In my heart, I resigned, then and there, though I held my silence for the moment as I sat before the board of elders of the church.

That very night the Sunday evening church service had been joyous and positive for once. I stepped out and took a chance. I departed from traditional procedure and tried something that involved everyone.

We decided to change the format from the traditional song service, announcements, prayer, and sermon format to a more informal kind of a gathering. We were holding services in the local American Legion Hall. So having arrived early, my wife and I arranged the chairs in a circle rather than in a row. Rather than using the hymnal, we worshiped the Lord in singing choruses. Then we went into a time of prayer. And many people who had been bound were able to open up and pray. It was a very special experience for them. And then of course I shared in a more informal way from the Word of God, sitting there and teaching, more as I would within an intimate home fellowship rather than the traditional church setting.

It was electric. A lot of people got excited. But the board members had difficulty with the change of format. They were so upset they called a board meeting immediately after the service. The irony was that I had started this church. Yet the incorporating officers had not even made me an officer on the board. I was put more in the role of a hireling. Since they all had strong denominational backgrounds, they made sure that the church constitution and rules of order were virtually the same as those of a denominational church. Now, after this exciting service, they informed me that they did not want this to continue.

It seemed that our church, like so many churches, was artificially bound by extrabiblical rules and formalities, and run by men who acted as employers rather than brethren bonded together in the love of Christ. Elders, so often, were voted into those positions because they were successes in the secular world. They had prestige or money. And so it was by worldly standards that they were usually chosen. If they had succeeded pragmatically in business, people reasoned, then why couldn't they help the church? It was a worldly formulation of success and had little to do with the standards of eternity. In fact, these very people can be the most inept when it comes to spiritual values and commitment because they have rooted their lives in outward success. If asked to sacrifice some of their affluence for the sake of Christ, I imagine that, like the rich young ruler, many of them would shake their heads and walk away. In our day, the Madison Avenue approach to church procedure has been sacralized.

Thus, the elders on the board used their rules of procedure to shape and confine the church to their own image; little wonder it lacked the explosive dynamism, relevance, and love of the early Church as reported in the New Testament. It seemed that we in the Church lost something on the way as these past twenty centuries went by. This, unfortunately, even applies to doctrinally conservative and "safe" churches. They so often follow a codified form of godliness but do not evince the true power thereof.

As I sat before the church board that evening I kept my composure and, rather than stir up dissent, I acquiesced to their request, not even seeking to defend what I had done. But in my heart burned a quiet certainty that God had called me to be a shepherd, not a hireling, or a ministerial employee on the payroll of businessmen.

I realized at that moment that this was not going to be my permanent place of ministry. It was the final move that solidified my decision to leave that rapidly growing fellowship and start all over again with the Bible study class I had in the Newport area. And the tiny fellowship at Calvary Chapel was already pressing me to come down and start my ministry with them. What was attractive in this was the opportunity to establish bylaws and articles allowing me freedom to be the shepherd responsible before God that I was called to be. Never again would I be a hireling of men, I vowed in my heart.

Still, I faced uncertainty. If it were my decision alone,

this costly choice would not have been nearly so bad. But naturally it involved my wife as well. And I knew my decision would jolt her like an earthquake. Seventeen times she had had to follow me and move to a different location. For seventeen years she had seen me work to supplement my ministry income. I had anything but a track record that would bring confidence and hope into the heart of a wife. Finally, I had worked up to a respectably sized church that was growing monthly. And only recently we had purchased a lovely new home that she loved. Now this brief oasis for her, after seventeen years of wilderness wandering, would once again be snatched away from her and replaced with an uncertain future. It was almost cruel. But the critical factor for me was that I was certain that God had ordained my choice and my move. I had no choice but to tell her.

As usual in the churches I pastored, including that most recent church, Kay formed deep emotional bonds with the people. She could not understand how I could consider leaving this blossoming fellowship that we had started, that loved us so deeply, in order to go to a small struggling church, a church that was floundering and considering closing up shop. Not only that but, officially, I would be the associate pastor. I wouldn't even be the senior pastor.

"Are you sure this is the will of the Lord?" she asked me in emotional disbelief. Finally after a great deal of prayer, Kay looked me in the face. Her eyes shone like Abraham's Sarah, for she was willing to follow me anywhere. God used her to break my heart before him. This had to work, I pleaded before God with passion, though I knew God's leading was too strong for something not to be in the wind. By outward standards my move was insanity. How true that often is when faith is required.

TRIALS OF FAITH

Many years before the above-mentioned board meeting took place, I still had ahead of me seventeen years in the desert. A period that seemed to be mainly one of spiritual and financial drought. And had I entertained even the remotest inkling that God might have ahead for me the scope of ministerial harvest that exists today, I would have thought it presumption, a dreamer's fantasy, and no more. I might have laughed if you told me what lay ahead, but not out of faith.

Real faith involves giving glory to God before you see any sure evidence. The Lord, I'm afraid, nailed me on this one. Years before I had pastored a church in Corona. After two years of hard work—I prayed, and I visited door to door, I printed all kinds of fliers, and tried every program in the church growth manual—our membership of twenty-five dropped to seventeen, five of whom were members of my own family! So it was necessary for me to work in a secular job in order to support our needs. God graciously opened up a job for me with Alpha Beta Market. I had a great deal. Since I managed the produce department, I could go in at four in the morning and get off at two in the afternoon. That left the afternoon and evening for my ministry.

When we received word that my wife's mother died in Phoenix, we got someone to take the church for us and notified the manager there at Corona that we were going to be gone for a couple of weeks to take care of the funeral and wind things up on that end. By the time I got back to Corona, I went in to report for work and my name wasn't on the board. I found the manager and said, "Well, I'm back now and ready to go to work." And he said, "There is a problem. You're going to have to go over and check with the union. You are behind on your dues. They said you cannot go back to work until you are paid up on your back dues."

I went over to the union to pay my back dues. And they said, "Well, you've been late so there's an assessment of a fifty dollar fine." I explained about the death in the family. They said it was too bad. Then I said that unless I was working I wouldn't even have the money to pay the fine. They replied that I could not work until I had paid the fine. And so it went, back and forth. It was a standoff, and they won.

And so without that money coming in we soon started to get notices that our payments were overdue. Meanwhile, the Alpha Beta Market had been wanting me to go into management. You don't have to belong to the union if you are in management. They had made an attractive offer to me, a very lucrative offer, to go into market management. But their one requirement was that I no longer try to pastor a church. The president, Claude Edwards, was a former minister. They liked my work, and they liked ministers, but I would have to give up the ministry and make marketing a career.

And I thought . . . well, I was getting behind in my debts and I really hadn't had much success pastoring; the church was going down. Maybe God had called me to be a businessman. Maybe I ought to forget the ministry and go into marketing. It sounded like a fine career. And with the bills mounting up and all of the things we needed for our small children, maybe this was a new door opening for us.

One morning I was so worried about the bills and what we were going to do that I couldn't go back to sleep. I was tossing around and worrying. I didn't want to wake up Kay, so I rolled out of bed quietly and went on out into the living room and sat there. Then I opened up the desk drawer and I got out the bills and totaled them all up. It came to four hundred and sixteen dollars. And I thought, *Well, that's it. I can't go on any longer in the ministry. I'll just have to forget it. I'll go in today and talk to them about a marketing career.*

When the rest of the family got up, Kay fixed breakfast. Then, as I was watching our beautiful children, the phone rang. I answered the phone and when the caller asked how I was doing I responded, in a robust voice, "Oh, great. How are you doing?"

Now I made a covenant with the Lord when I went into the ministry. I told Him I would never let anybody know my financial problems. I would never ask people for money. I would never ask them to give money to the church. I would never take a second offering. I vowed at the time, "Lord, I'll never make money an issue; I will never let people know my personal needs. And I won't poor-mouth God's providence saying, 'Oh, boy, we're having such a terrible trial this month. The kids need tennis shoes . . .' " and so on. None of that stuff. I wasn't going to insult my Boss by complaining about the wages.

After I told the caller that I was doing great he replied, "The Lord has been laying you on our hearts, and so we sent you a check yesterday special delivery. It should get there probably sometime today. We just thought we would let you know so you would be watching out for it."

And I said, "Oh, praise the Lord, that's really wonderful of you to do that. Thank you so much." He said, "It's for four hundred and twenty-six dollars." I hung up the phone, went into the kitchen, grabbed hold of my wife, and waltzed her around the kitchen, praising God. "It's all right, honey. We'll be able to pay every bill we have. And we'll even have enough money to go out to dinner. Lord, You're so great! Thank You, Lord, thank You. How good You are. What a blessing."

After about an hour or so, when I finally began to settle down a bit the Lord began to speak to my heart. He said, *What are you so excited about?* And I kept burbling thank You's to Him. He said, *How do you know they are going to send that money?* I said, "Come on, Lord, You've got to be kidding. These people have been friends for a long time. They are good people. I trust them. They wouldn't call me up and tell me something like that unless they had sent it. Their word is good, Lord."

Then He got me. He said, *This morning when you got up, you couldn't sleep. You were moping around. Now you had My Word that I would supply your needs. And I didn't see you waltzing your wife around the kitchen. I didn't see you exuberant and praising Me. Now that you have gotten the word of man, you are all excited. Whose word do you really trust more?*

What a lesson! "Lord," I said, "I'm sorry that I didn't trust Your Word more." If I had really trusted God at four A.M. I would have announced to Kay, "Look here at Philippians 4:19: God's going to supply all of our needs according to His riches in glory. Praise the Lord."

God was not being harsh at all, but in profound love He was teaching me a life-changing lesson. For if He is not there for us *always* our lives are sheer futility, and it is only a matter of time before the fantasy melts and we are utterly alone in the universe. Trust cannot be partial. It is all or none. Christ's lessons on faith were identical. Peter walking on water. Having the faith of a child. Simple, direct belief. Period. This lesson also prepared me for what God had ahead for me, though I would never have guessed it then. I had to learn to be faithful in the little things. I had to learn, as Abraham did, that what God has promised He is also able to perform.

My eyes had been off of God and on my problem and it had grown bigger and bigger. But if I had gotten my eyes back on God, then the problem would have grown smaller and smaller. Abraham's faith enabled him to give glory to God before he saw any sure evidence. This was an important lesson.

A MOST UNLIKELY PROPHECY

During the era when I was still a member of a denominational church, a group of us would meet for prayer together. One of us would sit in the chair and the group would lay hands on him and pray. As I was sitting in the chair with the group praying for me, there came a word of prophecy in which the Lord said that He was changing my name. The new name He was giving me meant "Shepherd," because He was going to make me the shepherd of many flocks and the church would not be large enough to hold all of the people who would be flocking to hear the Word of God.

Then there was another prophecy that followed some years later. The discouraged group down at Calvary Chapel had met to determine whether to call me here to minister or to disband. As they were praying, a word of prophecy came to them that I was going to come, that I would seek to remodel the church immediately, that I would be remodeling the platform area especially, that the church was going to be crowded to where it could not contain all of the people. That it would then have to move to the bluff overlooking the bay. That it would develop a national radio ministry, and would become known around the world. A more unlikely prophecy could not have been uttered to sixteen discouraged people ready to quit and throw in the towel.

I have learned through all these things that God is working out a foreordained, prearranged plan. He is directing every turn and facet of my life, if I will only look to Him for guidance. Sometimes, because I do not understand the difficulty I am facing, I must look through the eyes of faith. And through faith I must realize that all things are working together for good. But then as I look back I can see that the hand of God was leading me and directing me into various things. It is so beautiful to trace His hand in my life—even though sometimes He was directing me into a move that was not an easy or comfortable situation, but He needed to teach me some lessons.

Sometimes when I moved, God was teaching me not to move without being directed. And so He let me make that move to show me the danger of going ahead without His direction. But even then I can see the hand of God as He was working out His perfect plan in my life. He knew what it would take to bring me to Himself. He knew the circumstances it would take to bring me to a complete commitment of myself to Him. And then He knew what it would take to bring me to the end of myself, where I would give up totally and completely, reckoning my old self to be dead. And God knew exactly what it would take, circumstantially, to bring this transition about in my life.

God also knew the work He planned to do through me to touch the lives of others. He knew and foreordained the work I was to accomplish for His glory that would have a rippling effect until it reached around the world. Before

He could work through me, He had to work in me, conforming me by His Spirit into His image, bringing me into the measure of the stature of fullness of Christ. Once He had accomplished His work in me, He could then do all of those things He was desiring to do through me.

I do not believe that I have fully apprehended that for which He appointed me, nor do I feel His work in my own character is complete. I still have a long way to go before I fully reflect the image of Christ! But thank God His work continues as He is changing me from glory to glory.

The Bible speaks of those who despise the days of small things. I know I was often upset in the days of preparation. Indeed I still get impatient with God. But God is preparing me for that work He has up ahead for me. God was, and still is, working in my life to condition me for that next step, whatever it might be. For we are His *poema*, His workmanship or work of art. God desires to express Himself in the lives of his people. We become the expression of God to the world, for it is through what they observe in us that they get some idea about the nature and character of the One who fashioned us, the Artist. Thus God seeks to reveal Himself through me and through all genuine believers.

As I submit to God's touch, He is able to express His poetry in and through me. This is a staggering thought, and an immense responsibility. And without His grace, it is impossible.

3

As Far As the Eye Can See

In the wilderness of Galilee, where the plains meet the mountains folding in upon them, there is a beautiful but brief phenomenon. For just a few days every year, beginning one early spring morning, you can look out on what had been a plain, and see a meadow covered with a canopy of wildflowers extending as far as the eye can see—poppies, lilacs, buttercups, all radiating color and dancing in the wind. It literally happens overnight.

One morning Kay and I looked out into the California streets and on the beaches, and we beheld another radiantly colorful sight: human forms, extending as far as the eye could see. The countercultural revolution of the '60s had begun, and the new citizens were the hippies, "heads," and trippers. Their colorful outfits belied the deeper problem that they represented. If God was trying to tell us something, as we looked out on that field, we faced the problem of a gap of culture and thought that stood between our generations. I was brought up in old-world piety compared to the fast-track rebellion of the hippies. How could my wife and I cross this gulf?

The Lord pressed it on our hearts clearly, *Reach out in love*. Now we knew that love could never be contrived with a group as sensitive and perceptive as that one. So, to quote my wife, we saturated the air with prayers. She organized late-night prayer groups and morning prayer groups. It seemed that Kay and her friends were praying all the time. Meanwhile I prayed with elders and some church members. Before too long, we both felt a quiet change in the air, an excitement just beneath the surface.

Kay and I could feel it growing inside our hearts, almost independent of our own efforts—a growing burden of love and concern from God for these young people. With love, we believed, would come the necessary understanding. Then we might be equipped to minister to the real needs of these estranged youths. Could this be what God had been preparing us for all these years? Were we looking at fields rich with harvest, dislocated souls ripe for almost anything from Buddha to Christ, and only waiting for the chance to give themselves over? The cultural shift had happened quickly between our generation and theirs, like the wildflowers suddenly appearing on the Galilean plains. How could we penetrate it?

Kay and I would often drive to a coffee shop in Huntington Beach and park our car. We would sit and look at those kids and pray for them. Where others seemed to be repulsed by these dirty long-haired "freaks," we could only see the great emptiness of their hearts that caused them to turn to drugs for the answers to life that we knew only Jesus could supply. But how to reach them?

Then one day it happened. We met several youths who were hippies, yet they had a different glow on their faces. They were Christians, converted in San Francisco's Haight Ashbury district through a communal ministry called The House of Acts. They were perfect representatives of their generation, having been to all the "Human Be-Ins" in Golden Gate Park, Grateful Dead Concerts, "acid tests,"

Merry Pranksters events, Whole Earth Festivals, and communal experiments. They had done it all. Then one day they saw the bottom of the elevator shaft within their own souls. They glimpsed the ultimate emptiness of their pursuit, and finally called upon Christ to be the center and Lord of their lives.

We invited a couple of these youths to move into our home with us in Newport Beach. They soon moved some of their friends in as well, and it became sort of a communal house for a while. Our four kids accepted them and we began to understand their disillusionment with the church and the adult world that they called the Straight Society. They had lost all faith in any truths that had preceded their generation. They took it upon themselves to find newer and higher spiritual truths and begin a revolution.

But in their rootlessness, they were supremely vulnerable. Without history they operated from out of a vacuum. They were like medieval peasants going into the sophisticated center of London, naïve people open to being conned by slick street sellers and card tricksters. They denied the powers of darkness while they trafficked in the occult. Yet the devil loves occultists who deny him, as C. S. Lewis shrewdly observed.

As the numbers of converts grew, we realized that we had to find a place for these converted hippies to live. For we could not send them back to the hippie communes, knowing that they were not yet strong enough to resist the temptations of free sex and drugs that abounded there.

We started establishing Christian communal houses to hold them. The initial house elders came from the group that Kay and I had put up for a while. Their own zeal was contagious as they shared the rich truths of their new-found faith. By their zealous sharing about Jesus to those on the beaches, in the parks, and on the streets, they filled the area with the reality and doctrine of Christ. As we will see in detail when I discuss the lives and ministries of Greg Laurie, Jeff Johnson, Steve Mays, Mike MacIntosh, and others, this urgent and timely ministry took off like a rocket. It was irrepressible. God put to use people whose lives had been a social engineer's nightmare. And my wife and I witnessed this miracle time and again.

OVERCOMING BARRIERS OF PREJUDICE

Ironically, the only damper we encountered came from the church itself, those from our midst who had grown up with church backgrounds, those from the "Straight Society." This sudden infusion of rebellious youths met predictable resistance.

Our challenge was to overcome what most churches had not: namely, their insistence on respectability, conformity, and a judgmental attitude toward anything that departed from the norm. Many of our members rallied to the challenge, feeding off the zeal of the hippie converts. But there were still some who resisted and disdained these newest members of our church who showed up with long hair, bells on the hems of their jeans, bare feet, and who otherwise looked like wildflowers in their great diffusion of dress inspired by American Indian or Asian tribal styles. It was wildly creative. But it was also threatening, especially to those with young children who did not want them emulating the hippies.

The interesting thing is how we saw love prove itself as God's adhesive force time and again. Duane Hart, a man who today is one of our elders, is a good example of the resistance many felt. He was furiously suspicious of the hippie converts. He felt that they were insincere freeloaders and manipulators who were unable to change; never would they be able to work and support themselves.

Then one afternoon as Duane was working side-by-side with a group of hippie converts—at the time we were dismantling the school building that had not been up to code—Duane saw something that pierced his heart. These lean, muscular young men worked tirelessly as they sweated away in the summer sun pulling off the old roof tiles. Long hours went by and they never slowed down. By the end of the day Duane finally noticed, as they were scrubbing down piles of old roof tiles for use on the new structure, that their hands were bleeding they had worked so hard. And with their hands bleeding, these young men worked 'way into the night, singing of their newfound love for Jesus. God so convicted Duane of his judgmentalism that by the end of the day, there was not a word he could utter about them except in their defense from then on.

On another occasion, a renowned surgeon came to Calvary Chapel at the invitation of his future son-in-law, Don McClure. Don is another Calvary Chapel pastor whom I will be mentioning in this book. As Dr. Anderson told us later, he had had utter contempt for the hippie movement, and the morning he came to Calvary Chapel he was very ill at ease in the packed crowd. As much as he may have tried selectively to ignore these zealous converts, they were everywhere.

Rigid as a board, the illustrious surgeon mouthed the hymns. When it came time to read a passage of Scripture corporately, behold, this world-renowned man had no

Bible. But sure enough, someone near him did, a tall, shaggy, straggle-haired hippie. Reluctantly, condescendingly, he accepted the Bible, perhaps the way a Pharisee might take something from someone ceremonially unclean. As he opened it, he noticed that it had apparently been read with avid devotion, as Scriptures were underlined, starred, colored with felt-tip markers, and notes were scrawled in the margins. Shame and conviction flooded him. By the end of the service something in him changed.

But it really came down to my having to make a statement to men like Duane and some of our older members from straight church backgrounds. It was an issue that could have destroyed our work if we did not head it off. I told them:

"I don't want it ever said that we preach an easy kind of Christian experience at Calvary Chapel. But I also do not want to make the same mistake that the Holiness Church made thirty years ago. Without knowing it, they drove out and lost a whole generation of young people with a negative no-movie, no-dance, no-smoke gospel. Let us at Calvary not be guilty of this same mistake. Instead, let us trust God and emphasize the work of the Holy Spirit within individual lives. It is exciting and much more real and natural to allow the Spirit to dictate change. Let us never be guilty of forcing our Western Christian subculture of clean-shaven, short-hair styles or dress on anyone. We want change to come from inside out. We simply declare that drugs, striving to become a millionaire, or making sports your whole life is not where true fulfillment or ultimate meaning lies. Because the end of all these goals is emptiness and disappointment."

Perhaps this involves interesting symbolism, but I think

that the last barrier to go in our church was the "bare feet" barrier. When we got beyond that, we were home free. The pivotal incident centered on a wide expanse of brand-new carpet that we had just put in. Those who had been inwardly protesting the hippies finally found a target to vent their discontent upon: Dirty feet soil carpets, and these carpets cost a lot of money. Besides, who wants to see dirt marks on a brand-new carpet? They took it upon themselves, early one Sunday morning, to hang up a sign reading, *No bare feet allowed.*

For some reason I happened to reach the church earlier than usual, and was in time to take down the sign. It was sad to see division over things this trivial. It was also sad to see what really lay behind the outward demarcations of division: a we/they polarity instead of love. This time, I was the one to call the board meeting, and I would not be overwhelmed in the manner that I reported earlier. Now, not only was I on the board, but I was president of the corporation. This did not make me a dictator by any means, but it meant that I would be free to be God's man with a clear conscience, and I would not be in a hireling status.

Then I spoke from my heart to the board:

"In a sense it is we older established Christians who are on trial before the young people. We are the ones who told them about James 2 and 1 John 4:7. The kind of action we displayed today puts, as James said, a question mark across our faith. When this happens we have to ask ourselves who or what it is that controls and guides our motives.

"If because of our plush carpeting we have to close the door to one young person who has bare feet, then I'm personally in favor of ripping out all the carpeting and having concrete floors.

"If because of dirty jeans we have to say to one young person, 'I am sorry, you can't come into church tonight, your jeans are too dirty,' then I am in favor of getting rid of the upholstered pews. Let's get benches or steel chairs or something we can wash off. But let's not ever, ever, close the door to anyone because of dress or the way he looks."

Calvary Chapel jumped over that last hurdle. We were ready to move ahead.

HARVEST FIELD AFTER HARVEST FIELD

Before too long, I was sending people out to plant other churches, other Calvary Chapels, in other parts of California as well as other parts of the country. Many of the people we sent out were youth extracted from the very counterculture that our "no bare feet" barrier would have prohibited. What a tragedy that would have been if we had closed the doors on them! I am sure that the flow of God's grace would have gone from a gush to a trickle if we had been that shallow.

If after all my years of struggle in God's crucible, I had not learned the lesson of following God's way above man's way or the way of church tradition, and learned to offer Christ's love instead of respectability and conformity, I like the salt would have been worthy, from God's perspective, of being cast upon the road to be trodden under foot. For I believe in God's eyes that I as a servant would have lost my "saltiness."

Instead, I saw the Calvary Chapel explosion of grace rise beyond my wildest dreams. Costa Mesa planted numerous Calvary Chapels, many of which have attendance that numbers in the thousands. Several of them, not too far from Costa Mesa, number over seven thousand apiece. And the great work of God's design that I see here is that He has chosen as His ministers men who at one time were absolutely hopeless by society's standards. Their backgrounds embody virtually every depravity of our culture. And with almost perfect irony, the buildings that they have moved their churches into also embody almost every focal point that our society as a whole has retreated to as it has abandoned the church.

My son, Chuck, Jr., observed, when he moved his Capo Beach Fellowship into the sizable Capistrano Beach bowling alley, "We have gone to where the people are, and we have taken over their hangouts. Now when they go to our beautifully refurbished church, they are going to where they used to spend Friday and Saturday nights bowling."

What are these buildings that we have moved into? Raul Ries took over a Safeway store in West Covina; Don· McClure took over an orange-packing house in Redlands; Mike MacIntosh first invaded one of the largest movie theaters in San Diego, then moved into a public school facility; Jeff Johnson took over one of the largest chain store facilities in the country; Steve Mays took over a similar discount house; and Greg Laurie was our one big exception: He built a massive structure designed to hold close to four thousand a service. Indeed, these were the only structures available that could contain the numbers turning out. Now Calvary Chapel churches extend to Philadelphia and upstate New York. And some of these have even grown to more than a thousand in regular attendance.

God has opened the floodgates and shown us harvest field after harvest field. We have learned that if we do not erect any barriers, and if we surrender our lives to Christ's purpose, there seems to be almost no limit to His grace. I watch this, and I stand back amazed. A day does not pass that I do not rejoice in my heart and thank God from the very bottom of my heart. It makes every moment of my desert years worth it, and I can say with the apostle Paul, "For I reckon that the sufferings of this present time are not worthy to be compared with the glory which shall be revealed in us." I have been very fortunate to see some of these fruits in my own lifetime, especially when much greater men such as Abraham believed far greater promises and yet saw almost no sign of their fulfillment in their own lifetimes.

Now I can see, looking back, that all of these moments in the wilderness of my life that had seemed so hopeless, when my nose was pressed against the rock of despair, were worth every moment of blind struggle. God was teaching me and preparing me for His harvest by His own timetable and logistics, not mine! I could never have seen it in a million years when I was at that church of seventeen wondering whether or not God wanted me to stay in the ministry. I am thankful that His ways are not our ways, nor are His thoughts our thoughts. He can do far more through us than we would ever allow ourselves to dream.

4

Greg Laurie: From Five Earthly Stepfathers to One Father in Heaven

As I responded to the ringing doorbell of our home in Newport Beach, I looked at a sight that had become quite familiar to us. A young man with long hair, bare feet, shining smile, and clear eyes had his hand outstretched as he said, "Hi, I'm Greg." He had just come from Harbor High School, which was just around the corner from our house.

He handed me a set of drawings that he said he had done that day in his art class. There, in cartoon form, were twenty-two illustrations of my message given the previous Sunday. I had spoken on the text from John 7:37 in which Jesus promised living water to the thirsty world if it would just come to Him and drink. I had shared how the thirst Jesus referred to was a spiritual thirst that everyone had for God, and pointed out the folly of trying to fill that thirst with physical things or emotional experiences. The sermon was concluded by showing that God not only fills the thirsty life, but that His Spirit will begin to gush forth out of the believer's heart and life like a river of living water.

The first picture in the series of cartoons was of a little hippie character in ecstatic joy with a fountain springing out from his heart. I was struck by Greg's perception and how he had so completely absorbed the message and so graphically portrayed its truth in the little cartoons. Greg saw my absorption in his work, and then asked in a hesitant voice, "Do you like it?" I cried back heartily, "I love it. We need to publish this."

We had been looking for a tract the kids could pass out that would appeal to the kids on the street, one that they would not take politely, then wad up and toss away. Soon, we were off to the local quick print shop and had 10,000 copies run off. A large group of volunteers spent the afternoon cutting them into pages as others stapled them together. That night all 10,000 tracts were handed out on the streets by some of our eager kids. Demands for more tracts came in immediately from areas where the tracts had found their way. We ultimately printed more than half a million of these tracts.

Today Greg Laurie pastors one of the largest churches in California—indeed, one of the largest churches in the United States. It is a conservative estimate to say that nine thousand different people go through the doors of his church, Harvest Fellowship, every week.

As you glimpse the enormous facility approaching it along the outskirts of Riverside, California—it is reminiscent of some aeronautical assembly plant towering above the condominiums near the Kennedy Space Center—you might be surprised to hear Greg tell you that this entire ministry was a "hand-me-down" nobody else wanted. By God's grace alone it grew into the ministry it is today. Greg is careful to tell you that it is God's church and not his.

And in Greg himself, God has turned around a life that was once bent in half by one of the worst curses of our culture, divorce. God often confounds the religious pundits of our day by using broken lives in a mighty role.

Divorce is a national sin that has marred one family after another, literally tearing this God-ordained institution in half. Children who have lived through one divorce know well enough what haunting loneliness it can create. They also know what real alienation is like—from themselves, from parents, from stepparents, and from friends.

Imagine, if you will, someone who has endured several of these parental splits and remarriages, someone who has grown up with his mother and as many as five stepfathers. No one could accuse such a person of being naïve about divorce, or inexperienced in the area of loneliness and pain. Surely, this person could stand up as a representative of his entire generation and say, "I know what it is like. I have lived through it five times." To overcome this crippling stigma is also to overcome, by the grace of God, one of the most evil social plagues to hit our world. Greg Laurie knows, because he is that very man.

When Christ entered Samaria, he met a woman at the well. As a Jewish rabbi, he broke tradition and shocked her by initiating conversation. He stunned her even more by offering her eternal life. And then He completely revealed the vastness of His grace by acknowledging that He was well aware of the fact that she had been "married" to five other men and the man she was living with was not her husband. Apparently she had a need that drove her and drove her, but she never seemed to find fulfillment.

What does this mean for us today? For people like Greg who have suffered from broken homes? If this woman had

had a son, I imagine he could cross the twenty centuries of time between them and meet eyes with Greg Laurie, his modern counterpart. With the props of civilization removed, their emotional experiences would be very much the same. Such are the timeless effects of sin. Neither time nor custom can change them; only grace can remove them. This is what Greg Laurie learned. It was a hard but life-saving lesson, one that he now can share with others.

THE TRAUMA

It seemed like any other school day for nine-year-old Greg. In a few minutes the bell would ring and he planned to run outside and play in New Jersey's autumn air. He liked to chase leaves about in the wind on the way home. Leaves didn't fall off trees in sunny Southern California, where he was born in 1952, as they did here in New Jersey. In fact there were hardly any seasons at all in California.

The move East had meant a big change for Greg, but he had settled into a happy and contented lifestyle. He was basking in the stability and security that he had yearned for over the years. Greg liked his latest stepfather, Oscar Laurie, whom he had come to think of as his real father, the dad he always wanted. Oscar, an intelligent and successful New York lawyer, had always shown Greg genuine kindness and affection. And when Greg needed it, this man of consistency and integrity gave him appropriate discipline. After a string of three other stepfathers Greg finally felt secure.

The bell rang and Greg fired out the school door amidst a swarm of kids and led the charge toward the street.

Suddenly his frenzied excitement came to a halt. Greg spotted a sleek black Cadillac limousine pulling up in front of the school. He had an unsettling feeling of dread in the pit of his stomach as if he were watching a movie of his life and the image was starting to flicker. He walked slowly toward the street. The dread nearly choked him when he saw his mother inside the car. Then he noticed the boxes. Was he about to reexperience a painfully similar scene?

Greg approached the car. "What's going on?" His mom responded matter-of-factly, "We're leaving."

"Where are we going?"

"We're going to Hawaii."

Then, through waves of fear, the movie image flickering badly, he asked, "Well, where's Dad?"

"Dad's not coming." This pronouncement was abrupt and final. The pleasant movie that had once been his life was over. And he had no idea what the next movie script of his life would be.

En route to Kennedy Airport, Greg cried the entire way. And during the long, agonizing flight to Hawaii, Greg reviewed in his mind the parade of faces that had stood in as his dad.

The sense of hopelessness was magnified when Greg saw the next man to enter the role of stepfather. He didn't like this new one standing at the gate at Hawaii's airport, a big rough-cut fellow. This man's face didn't have the tender honesty of Oscar's. He seemed hard, smooth. Greg's mom, a stunning Marilyn Monroe look-alike whom men had pursued as far back as Greg could remember, stepped into the picture like a seasoned actress. The Hawaiian setting, by all outward appearances, was idyllic, but Greg only saw ugliness. He wanted with all his heart to be back with Oscar Laurie.

They got into a flashy new car and drove up to an opulent house. This new man in his mother's life, Al, was rich. He even had a swimming pool. Soon, Al led them proudly down the hall to Greg's new room.

When Greg stepped into his new room, he felt the mocking brunt of a bad joke. It was identical, right down to the last detail—toys, wall color, shelving, and position of the bed—to his room back in New Jersey at Oscar's house. Greg felt betrayed. Never again, he resolved in his heart, would he trust the adult world. It was a hard world of deceivers whose smiles always seemed to belie their motives.

Greg also decided at that moment that he would have to adapt to this world of hardball if he was going to survive. If life was just a ruthless game, he would need to be very cunning. At the doorway of his new room, Greg passed a turning point in his life. From then on rebellion became a way of life. He decided that the qualities of virtue, truth, and goodness, which he had once longed for, now seemed to be relegated to fairy tales, forever taunting with false hope. Whenever they appeared, they vanished like wisps of clouds when he got near. He had always believed in God in his heart, but God seemed to be too distant.

Al let Greg do anything. He could spent the day running up and down Waikiki beach, while Al and his mom spent the day at Al's plush hotel bar. Alcohol was a big part of their life. Whereas Oscar had made Greg earn any money beyond his fixed allowance, permissive Al would hand out five dollar bills at the asking. On the outside, materially, things couldn't have been better. On the inside, Greg was empty. He had everything money could buy. Unfortunately, it couldn't buy love.

It also became plain in time that the marriage between

Al and Greg's mom was not made in heaven. Their fights became worse, at times loud and violent, as Greg lay awake in bed listening.

One evening Greg was in front of his house with a couple of friends when they heard a scream and a loud crash as a lamp went flying through the plate glass window. Soon the police arrived. Greg's mom also began to have black and blue marks.

Finally one night Greg heard loud screaming and yelling. He heard a forceful *whack* and found his mother lying on the floor with blood coming out of her head. He ran next door to the neighbors yelling that his mother was dying. The ambulance took her away. Remarkably, she lived. Al had hit her with a wooden statue. At that point the marriage died, and the two of them were back on the plane again, back to Southern California.

CHANGING IDENTITIES AND PEER GROUPS

By the time Greg entered the tenth grade—after several problem years in school—he had learned how to be "cool." His goal was to hang out with the seniors. He had a quick mind, good looks, maturity, and natural charm that made him popular with almost any peer group he set his sights on. At Corona Del Mar High School, an affluent school of rich kids, button-down collars, and collegiate haircuts, for an underclassman to be accepted by the seniors was quite a feat. Yet Greg's gift at cynical mockery kept him at the center of attention. Before long he was part of the most elite senior clique, which hung out at Senior Square, "the place to be." An advantage to having little supervision at home was that he could be out all night and nobody cared. Greg and his clique of seniors often drove out to the all-night parties in Palm Springs. Corona Del Mar High was still unscathed by the nation-wide youth rebellion of the late '60s, so pot was unheard of on campus. Their parties centered around grain alcohol, beer, whiskey sours, and Margaritas. They were yuppies before their time.

But soon enough, the challenge was over. Greg saw through the clique mentality that he had worked his way into, and it left him empty and bored. There was also the ever-present reality that it wasn't so much friendship that bonded the group together as it was members expediently using each other.

Greg started to feel about this peer group game the same as he did the adult world, a world he mistrusted and even hated. Was this conformity-minded clique of seniors any different from the adult society they would soon enter? Nor was Greg that interested in their recreational drinking. Liquor held little mystery for him. After all it had ruined his whole childhood; he had spent countless hours going in and out of bars looking for his mother.

When he reached the eleventh grade, Greg decided to try a new identity: he would drop his clean-cut look and become a "head." A friend persuaded Greg to enter Newport Harbor High School. Newport Beach was a major drug center of California, and this particular high school was famous for spearheading the countercultural drive. On Greg's first day there, he abandoned his colle-giate, button-down collar look for jeans and lengthening hair. He also tried pot, which was all over the school, from Mexican weed to Eukiah sensemilla.

In no time Greg was heavily into smoking pot with his new group of friends. They all got stoned three times a day. It was during this time that Kay and I had our first contact with Greg, though we didn't know him at the time. On school lunch breaks Greg and his friends would go to a house only a few blocks from where my family lived. Kay started to notice this motley crew laugh and joke as they walked past our house on their way back to school. Clearly they were on drugs. It was at this point that the burden we felt for the youth subculture became almost intolerable. And that was when Kay and I started to pray for God to open doors for us to reach this alienated generation.

One day a fellow offered Greg LSD. It was at Costa Mesa where Greg had been hired to join a team of laborers dismantling the carnival. Greg dropped the acid while he worked, and soon was entering a new "spiritual" world where everything seemed to have hidden meanings. Insights kept flashing into his mind. He even transcended the fact that he almost got killed by a crane: This was a mere cosmic love tap. Greg was beginning to smell eternity beneath the most ordinary things.

Greg had found a new purpose in life: the pursuit of truth through LSD. As an individualist he resisted blind conformity to the hippie movement. Though he looked like any other hippie, he insisted on having his own thoughts. For that reason he did not take part in Eastern religions, nature religions, "be-ins," or communes. Greg entered an open-ended era. And he loved LSD, which he took with his group regularly on weekends at friends' houses or in the California countryside.

Greg also began to notice a rather "uncool" group on campus. They were secure enough in their views not to care about social approval. They refused to conform to the new social revolution around them. In fact they were bolder than their extreme counterparts, the wildest rebels who defied all morality, standards, and institutions. The heat of conflict brought them out boldly, in this wildest of high schools. At lunch they often marched across the high school campus singing hymns and handing out tracts. Greg avoided them. They were Christians, the social lepers. The amazing thing about them was that a number had been in the dope scene much more deeply than Greg. Now they handed out tracts and smiled.

Every time Greg was handed a tract, he would look pointedly at the giver while sticking the tract into his back pocket. Greg had a drawer full of them. For some reason he never threw them away. And now and then he would get stoned, pull them out of a drawer, read them, and laugh. But his laughter got rather thin at one point as he found himself 'way over his head on LSD. He found himself in an unknown world. Greg discovered that it is a little hard to mock the abyss when you really don't know what lies at the heart of existence.

OPENING THE WRONG DOOR

It happened when Greg and a friend split a megadose of "orange sunshine" LSD. He lay down and waited to soar into some unknown realm. Greg was like someone with a pocket full of skeleton keys that could open one unknown door after another. It was the luck of the draw. Greg waited.

Suddenly the air rippled like water. A wave of insanity swept through him. He felt distinctly that he was losing his grasp on reality. And what lurked beneath was a feeling of evil—a sort of presence, if you will. Previously LSD had seemed to have a safety switch; you could always escape. It was like toying with a dangerous situation without suffering the consequences—almost like watching a movie at one of those massive cinemadome theaters. The illusion of being in the action is so great you begin to react. But there is always the release button of the movie ending. Your gut feels the rush of air and twirl of gravity as an F15 dives through a narrow canyon at a thousand miles an hour. But unlike the jet pilot, you won't get killed. You experience the thrill of being close to death without the consequences.

But was there always a safety valve on LSD? Greg had heard of people being killed by it or going insane. Could he be sure that he could bail out? What if the insanity did not go away? A new terror flooded him.

As he felt himself going berserk, he wanted to stand in front of a mirror, perhaps to recapture who he was and remember his identity. As he stared his face started to melt. It aged hideously, then it deformed with monstrous contortions. Then something jagged ripped through him, a hideous, pealing laughter. "You're gonna die, you're gonna die."

Greg ran outside and tried to rip his clothes off. Neighbors stared out through shuttered windows. Greg's friends grabbed him and held him. He kept thinking, *I'm in trouble, I need help. I may never get back to where I was.*

For months after that Greg felt that his brain was slightly fried. He realized that he did not want to take any more LSD. The stakes were too high.

IN THE PRESENCE OF THE LORD

Something drew Greg to the gathering crowd in the school cafeteria. The fellow speaking radiated joyous hope. He was in his twenties and had flaxen hair that went down to his shoulders. He looked like he had jumped out of a Bay Area billboard advertising Big Brother and the Holding Company at some Golden Gate Park Be-In. In fact, judging from his words, he had done it all. Now he had come to the end of his long search; he had come to the Lord. He was at Newport Harbor High that day to tell the kids about Jesus Christ, and why Christ, and not rock or acid, was the answer to every question they were asking. This fellow was still in the honeymoon of his own conversion experience and was feeling the thrill of it; it was infectious. So was his ability to evangelize boldly. Then he said something that caught Greg mid-track.

Greg had slipped into the back of the crowd. The last thing he wanted to be was a member of the "Jesus People," and become a social outcast. He had always believed in God, in the back of his mind, during private moments. Even as a small child Greg would quietly talk to God or say prayers to Him. And he noticed that often, when he got into tight situations, he would call out to God.

In fact quite recently Greg and his friends were speeding down the coastal highway outside of Laguna Beach late one night when it was raining. They had a kilo of pot in the trunk. Suddenly the car fishtailed wildly out of control. It looked certain that they would crash and die. Greg saw the headlines in his mind, "Drug Dealers Dead," after people found what was in the trunk. But he was never a drug dealer! What a terrible way to go. In a quick breath Greg spoke the prayer, "Oh, God, if You get me out of this I promise I will serve You." He had done this before with God and knew that God had come through every time. But

Greg would later retreat on his promises or conveniently forget them.

Now the words of Christ, spoken by the young man, suddenly cut into Greg: "You are either for Me or you are against Me." Greg never realized that. He always knew Christ was real, but he never knew that a choice of this nature existed—to be "for Him or against Him." Which was he? By not being "for Him," Greg was, in fact, in that great crowd against Christ. He had never realized you could be unwittingly against Christ. Apparently something was demanded of him, some kind of positive response. The speaker's eyes, at first mellow and loving, had become flint-like when he echoed Christ's words.

The speaker now challenged the hushed group to be "for" Him. Greg also noticed that a girl that he had liked from a distance for more than a year was one of "them," a Christian. He then began figuring what it would cost him to join "them." He squirmed inside because he sensed he would lose his newest identity and his latest group of friends. And what about his freewheeling lifestyle? He lived for himself, for fun. And surely he shouldn't be asked to make a fool of himself like these campus Christians.

But then there was another consideration eating away at Greg's mind. Because he had felt so betrayed as a child his highest allegiance had always been to find Truth at any cost. Could this have something to do with his search? Besides, what about that dark and terrifying encounter with LSD? What if, one day, one of these close brushes with insanity, death, or destruction slammed shut the safety valve permanently? Then that would be it. That would be the end of his life. What would his life have finally stood for then? Nothing noble or good, nothing to be proud of.

Greg Laurie made his decision for eternity right before the bell went off for fifth period. He came forward, bowed his head, and that was it. He asked God to forgive his sins and he asked Jesus Christ into his life to be his Lord and Savior. He cast his lot in to be with Christ. He was "for" Christ—finally. Greg also knew he had come to the end of his search. This was it, the Truth.

Before Greg knew it the pretty girl whom he liked threw her arms around him. People surrounded him and patted him on the back. It was wonderful. But now the peer wars would begin. How long could he hide what he had done? As it turned out, not too long. It was Friday and school was almost out. That meant it was time for his group to go off into the country for the weekend and get stoned.

Sure enough they went off on Ortega Highway in the wilds of nature near a national park. Someone offered Greg an acid tablet. He said no. He left them and went off alone to sit on a rock. Just as he was lighting up a pipe of grass, he felt the inner voice of the Holy Spirit speaking to his soul. He knew he would never smoke another one. Greg Laurie, that spring day of 1970, threw his stash away as well as his pipe. It was only a day after his conversion.

Like the words sung by Jeff Beck, Greg could say, "I have finally found a way to live, in the presence of the Lord."

A FAITHFUL WITNESS

Greg went to one of the houses where he and his friends had gotten stoned hundreds of times. He wanted to break it to them gently. In fact he left his Bible hidden in the hedge so that he could ward off their preconceptions. Then the mother of one of his drug buddies came through the front door with a smirk on her face and the Bible in her hand. "Whose is this?" When Greg explained to his pals what had happened to him they laughed and jeered. They also expressed disappointment. A good drug buddy was becoming a Jesus freak.

Every time Greg was put down or rejected by this or that peer group or friend, he realized how shallow those friendships had been and that he would not sway from his newfound faith. He became almost fanatical, and was soon out on the streets witnessing to people. Greg realized that it was an all-or-nothing commitment as far as he was concerned. It also began to dawn on him that, for the first time in his life, he had a purpose: It was not to live for himself, but to be a servant, a witness of his Lord. Within about two weeks of his conversion, Greg lost the last of his friends. Things were peeled away that quickly. Also, within that time, Greg started to go to Calvary Chapel.

Greg's first church experience as a Christian was at one of our evening services. It was in the smaller building right before we moved into the tent. Greg was momentarily overwhelmed by fear before going through the door. You see, part of the toll that having five stepfathers had extracted from his soul was a very real fear of intimacy, of the vulnerability that love requires. Greg visibly trembled at the door. Finally he squeezed into a front-row seat that a friend had been holding for him, and told me later that I was one of the first adults he was willing to trust. As I taught that night, Greg's heart went from mistrust and suspicion to trust. In no time he was attending every function we had, immersing himself in teaching and tapes. It seemed he couldn't get enough of it.

WHAT GOD CAN DO WITH A HAND-ME-DOWN

Greg had many negative hand-me-downs as a non-Christian youth, among them certain fears or insecurities. But he also had positive hand-me-downs once he was a Christian and was eager to minister. One of these was a Bible study. Greg went one night and the leader did not show up. No one else had much to say, so Greg started sharing what was on his heart. The host asked him to lead the Bible study the next week and from then on. By this time Greg had been attending Calvary Chapel for a few years.

Another situation helped point Greg toward the plans God had for his life. Greg showed up at Pirates Cove, Corona Del Mar Beach, to witness one of our Calvary Chapel baptisms. By 1972 we were baptizing around nine hundred a month. Greg arrived and no one was there. He thought he had gotten there too late. Then he saw a group of about thirty Christians singing together on the beach. He joined them, and as he did at the Bible study, Greg started sharing what was on his heart.

Soon two girls arrived and asked Greg if he was a pastor and if he could baptize them. Greg jumped up and said, "Oh, no, I'm not a pastor. I couldn't do that." But they were desperate. They felt that they had to be baptized then and there, and they were crushed that they had missed the Calvary Chapel baptism. They asked him again, and Greg assured them, "I'm not a preacher." Then he felt the voice of the Lord saying, *Do it.*

Greg turned to the others and said, "Well, these girls need to be baptized. So let's go down to the water and do it." He walked along the beach followed by thirty-two people and thought to himself, *What have I gotten myself into?* Greg wasn't sure he had all the words right, but he did it. After it was over, two more people showed up and asked to be baptized. And Greg baptized them as well.

Afterward Greg looked up at a rock bluff above him and saw a crowd of curious onlookers. He had already performed the sacrament of baptism; now he felt God telling him to preach. Greg stood below them and called up, "You may wonder what we are doing down here." When he was finished, a number of them gave their lives to Christ. God had just showed Greg another facet of his ministry: as preacher/evangelist. As it turned out, the Calvary Chapel baptism came hours after Greg was finished.

When Greg graduated from high school, he had a very strong sense that he was to remain around Calvary Chapel and not go on to college. During that time, he continued ministering and leading Bible studies and working on graphic arts. He was around the office all the time and did numerous things to help the staff as a self-described "gopher" eager to do anything. He would wait anxiously for the phone to ring when I was away, for the secretary would turn those calls over to him. I often wondered what some of those callers would have done if they had known that the person counseling them on the phone was a nineteen-year-old hippie.

The next hand-me-down that Greg received came when he was twenty years old, almost three years after he had become a Christian. There was a Bible study in Riverside that had once drawn three hundred people; now it had dropped to eighty. The problem came in finding someone to drive all the way to Riverside from Costa Mesa to lead it. My son, Chuck, Jr., had helped start and nourish it, but he felt called to start another church. After him, a string of leaders took it short-term. Then one day as a group was trying to find someone to lead it that week, and after everyone else had turned it down, they offered it to Greg.

Greg was eager to get any crumb that fell off the table, so he leaped at the opportunity. That dwindling Bible study in Riverside was the very fellowship that became the huge church Harvest Fellowship is today.

When Greg took the fellowship, attendance jumped back up to three hundred almost overnight. They shared the use of another church building, and young people flocked in. There were articles in the local papers about this phenomenon of counterculture youths turning to Christ and the dynamic leadership of Greg Laurie, who used Christian bands to lead praise songs along with other convention-breaking innovations. He was also traveling all over the country with evangelistic rallies.

As attendance grew Greg felt the Lord directing them to move into their own building. About a year after joining the fellowship he found a church building that was no longer in use and before long I was with Greg in the realtor's office. After I wrote out the down payment, I felt the thrill of telling Greg, "You just got yourself a church."

The fellowship of three hundred jumped to five hundred at their very first service. In one year they doubled in size. That necessitated multiple services.

By 1974 Riverside Calvary Chapel, as it was then called, met in the downtown Civic Center on Sunday evenings. It had 1,500 seats. Meanwhile they expanded their church building for the morning services. But by 1980, after five years of steady growth, Greg knew that they had to build a new building. The result was the colossal structure that towers over Riverside today with the big sign "Harvest

Christian Fellowship." Today, with three packed services on Sunday, they have more than 9,000 attending.

Greg has also been permitted by the Lord to go out and use his gift of evangelism. Recently he addressed an assembly of 10,000 in the Philippines, along with Raul Ries, whom you will meet later. Greg has shared what God has shown him about leadership at pastors' conferences in the U.S., Japan, Europe, and Africa. He also rented and filled a 1,000-seat auditorium in New York City, after being on the radio there for over a year. Many asked Greg afterward for a Calvary Chapel in New York City. The result is a Calvary Chapel in Manhattan that meets in a dance studio used by the Joffrey Ballet. It has already grown to three hundred members and is headed by Greg's old friend Mike Finizio, previously a Calvary Chapel pastor in Alaska. Greg is also on the radio in twelve metropolitan cities nationwide.

God, however, had an even more amazing plan in Greg's trip to New York. Someone from Greg's past who was very special to him was living in nearby New Jersey: one Oscar Laurie, the only man Greg ever considered to be his father. Greg went to see Oscar and introduced him to his pretty young wife, Cathe. He also got to do something else—and this is where we see God's incredible redemptive plan. Greg told him exactly what had changed his life—Jesus Christ.

Since Oscar had suffered a serious heart attack, he was beginning to weigh eternal values against temporal ones.

The next day Oscar said, "Greg, I thought about what you said last night. And I want to know what I must do to be saved and accept Jesus Christ into my life."

Greg again shared with Oscar the essence of the Gospel. Oscar replied, "I am ready to do it right now." They both knelt down and prayed. Oscar began to weep and then asked Greg if God could heal his heart. Greg blurted, "Yes."

Then Oscar, with the faith of a child, prayed for healing. In minutes, they were off to Oscar's doctor to prove to the doctor that Christ had touched him. Oscar had no doubts. And indeed, something had happened to Oscar physically. Today, Oscar Laurie is an elder in his church and his wife and two sons are all Christians. Greg looks at this—with everything else he has seen the Lord do in his life—with pure awe and gratitude.

As we have looked at the life of Greg Laurie, we have seen the story of a man who has had five stepfathers come to discover that he has had an eternal Father in heaven all along. Greg has realized that God has taken his weaknesses and flaws and turned them around to use them. Greg has also learned not to seek the approval of men, but of God. The huge numbers that his life has touched testify to Christ's promise of multiplying the numbers of sisters, brothers, mothers, and fathers He would add to our true family in Him.

Of particular joy to him was meeting Cathe, his wife. Her appearing in Greg's life has shown God's promise that if you seek His will, He will give you the desires of your heart that are according to His will. Greg had also been terrified of love. Now Cathe has provided him the love he always yearned for, a wholesome, loving, and stable family. And if you look at Greg and Cathe today, you learn—as opposed to what some psychologists declare—that with God's help, it is even possible for someone from a radically unstable family background to be blessed in marriage.

When it is all said, I am not sure which is the greater gift to Greg: the harvest of his ministry, or his marriage to Cathe and their two sons. Either way, God has worked a miracle that keeps increasing, like the loaves and the fishes, from a few hand-me-downs to the feeding of thousands.

5

Steve Mays: Hanging Out with the Outlaws from Killer Canyon to the Valley of Peace

One bleak day a hoodlum from Anaheim showed up at one of our Christian commune houses dressed in bib overalls and leathers, with a nine millimeter Baretta tucked in his back pocket. He had not bathed in six months and had literally slept in gutters while living as a fugitive from the law. He had not brushed his teeth in two years and, with his neo-barbarian hairstyle, he was a sight to behold.

His name was Steve Mays and he was alienated from everybody—from his parents, who had tossed him out of their house years before, to the motorcycle gang he had been living with, a tough group of bikers, a bunch of outlaws. He had been wanted by the FBI for attempted murder and draft dodging. There was also a contract out on his life.

Steve's path to destruction seemed clearly written on the wall from the time he was a child. He had been so uncontrollable that his parents resorted to calling the

75

police when things got out of hand, which was almost constantly by the time they threw him out of the house.

One of Steve's crowning acts at home, to follow a long line of bizarre events, took place one evening when he was home alone. When his parents returned, they had to shove open the front door; it had been wedged shut with towels. They discovered that their house had been made into a gigantic indoor bathtub. Water came gushing out the front door. Their son was sitting in the middle of the living room completely oblivious to the damage being done to his parents' house. He was smoking a pencil and tried to tell them about a TV show he was watching. The TV was off. He had been stoned for twenty-seven hours on yet another chemical. This time he had swallowed too much Asthmadore. He had experimented with more concoctions than you can imagine.

By the time the police arrived, his parents had gotten Steve to his room. Before his eyes his window hinges turned into toads and were apparently telling him jokes, making him laugh. When the police found out that Steven was a member of the Anaheim High School football team, they lectured him but did not arrest him.

By noon the next day Steve's father returned home early to have a look at his less-than-model son. This time Steve was in the kitchen fixing two place settings of milk and sandwiches. When asked who the other sandwich was for, Steve motioned to the clock on the wall and said it was for "Brad" who lived in the clock.

Not long after this episode Steve, stoned as ever—this time on LSD, hashish, and other drugs—terrorized his parents with a machete. His mother looked on in horror as Steve grimaced and paced around swinging the blade. Once he fell asleep, his bewildered parents took away the machete. To say the least, there was a considerable generation gap between Steve and his parents. His father was a lab technician and former military man and patriot. His '60s generation son had become impossible. In truth, the two had ceased communicating years before.

Looking back, Steve pinpoints one day in seventh grade when his life took a turn toward destruction. He came home from school changed, and everybody noticed the change, though they didn't know what had caused it. On that day, a respected authority figure, one of his teachers, had molested him homosexually. It was such a terrible encounter that Steve blocked it completely from memory for years. His behavior went awry from then on. In little time, while still in seventh grade, he was smoking pot and stealing. His grades went from straight *A*'s to *D*'s and *F*'s as his motivation went out the window. Life became one big game of hookey, pot, pills, speed, and beach parties. Steve was on a twisted slope downward.

By the time Steve was in high school, his stealing had become a serious problem. He was booked four times in one week. Then by the time of the machete episode, Steve quit the high school football team (his drug antics had been getting more and more inappropriate on the football field) and became the high school drug dealer. Steve and his football ex-teammates would smoke entire "lids" in a single joint. They could get any drug they wanted and tried them all.

On one weekend mountain retreat—Steve had planned to go but for some reason couldn't—some of the football players got so high on reds, barbiturates, that they overdosed. By the time their mountain cabin caught fire, they were unconscious, too "out of it" to move. All of them were killed and the tragedy shook the entire high school.

About this time Steve turned against his parents totally. He despised them. His hostile mood changes were further affected by changes in his body chemistry from taking "uppers" such as speed, dexedrine, and meth amphetamine. These uppers were now keeping Steve awake three and four days straight. He was becoming increasingly paranoid because of the lack of sleep. Doctors had no idea then what they know now about the metabolic cycles of these specific drugs. Meanwhile Steve had to find a way of releasing the fierce energy bursts that would come upon him. He would stay up all night whacking away with his hammers and tools on his newest project— overhauling his sports car. When his dad came home from work he would find his son in the driveway, banging away on the car at all hours of the night. Steve was dropping out of the world fast.

Steve's new dream was to be a terrorist. His rage caused him to be in fights at school constantly. He hit one fellow thirty-one times in the face. He cut off another guy's finger. By the time his orders to appear before the draft board came, Steve defiantly burned his draft card and went on the road. The only place left for him to go, as far as Steve's parents were concerned, was out the front door. They had an incorrigible rebel on their hands who was beyond hope.

A HEARTBEAT FROM HELL

Steve's new place of residence was in a section of Orange County known as Garden Grove, in the hangout of a motorcycle gang. Steve was able to stay as long as he applied his mechanical talents to motorcycle body work. But his fellow tenants were fierce masters. If his parents had been unloving or alienating at times, these new housemates were positively demonic. Steve discovered a terror that he never would have dreamed existed back on the old homestead. It seemed some sort of spiritual door had been thrust open that most people don't know about, or would never want to know about.

The motorcycle gang members were in their mid-thirties, twice Steve's age. They also carried guns and were heavily involved in crime and drug-dealing. As bad as Steve was, he was innocent compared to them. There was also another thing that differentiated Steve from them, and it may seem like a minor point, but it wasn't in their social world: they were into reds or "downers," while Steve was manically on "uppers." His frenetic binges got on the nerves of a few of them. One of them especially had it in for Steve and he began scaring Steve more and more with his guns, as Steve's first year of residency with them went into the second year. This became a source of terror as various incidents heightened what was a sadistic game.

I will let Steve Mays recount this era, as he has done often when giving his testimony:

"One night a motorcycle was tipped over. They woke up and said I did it. I would stay up all through the night and separate bolts and nuts and put them in absolute order. Then I would dump them all out on the floor and work through this same ritual again. That was how stoned I was. I would take twenty dexedrines at one time with ten cups of coffee. I would take the twenty dexies and crush them, I would add an Excedrin, a vitamin, and put it all in a horse pill and swallow it with coffee. I would get so wired my mind would just fry.

"So they woke me up early one morning after my binge

was over. They said that I had rolled the bike over. I told them I didn't touch it.

"The guy who had it in for me reached for something. Then I saw the blue barrels of a twelve-gauge double barreled shotgun. He told me to open my mouth while the others held me and helped shove it in my mouth. Then I said, 'That isn't loaded, is it?' They pulled it out, pointed at the pillow next to my ear, and pulled the trigger. It blew pillow feathers all over the place. Then they stuck the shotgun back in my mouth and smoke began to come out. I thought I was going to die. My paranoia really began to grow from then on. That's when another guy living there gave me his gun to protect myself. It was then that I started carrying a gun. I would have to stay awake all night to make sure that I wouldn't die, living in the same house with a guy who wanted to kill me.

"Soon after that I was out in the backyard working on my motorcycle. He came out in the yard with a thirty-eight pistol. I was sitting on a gasoline can as a chair, while I worked on the cycle. He shot three rounds into the bottom of the can. He missed me, and it was just by a miracle that the gas can did not blow up with me on it."

But Steve did not leave the house. He learned the lifestyle of his older mentors and became freewheeling with his new pistol. As the house began to sell more and more dope, Steve began to deal more. A girl who came by to get dope wanted to buy it from another guy and not Steve. This infuriated Steve, so when she walked away, he started firing his gun at her. But he was too stoned to hit her. The bullets flew over her head. Then the rage mounted. He now wanted to kill something, anything. The target became a cat.

"I shot this alley cat with a thirty-eight. It just smiled at

me after I shot it. Then I took a pitchfork and ran that
through the head. It still continued smiling at me. Then I
took a sledgehammer to it. And it still smiled. Finally I
took my thirty-eight, put it to the cat's head, and blew
what remained away. It rolled into a ditch and still smiled
at me. From that point on, every place I went there was a
cat. I think that was the closest I came to being demon-
possessed."

A member of the gang told Steve that someone had
taken a contract out on him. Steve had been working on
three motorcycles that he used. A shovel-headed Harley
Davidson 1200 cc Hog, a '49 Indian, and a Trike. But
where do you go when you don't even know who has the
contract out on you? Instead of running Steve got a
shotgun with a twelve-inch barrel and a pistol handle, and
began practicing with it in the garden, thirty and forty
rounds.

But one evening, at a time when Steve wasn't suspect-
ing anything, his old enemy who lived in the house pulled
out a thirty-eight pistol and pointed it at Steve. "I hate
you. There's a contract out on your head, and I may as
well collect on it as anybody else." Steve heard an
explosion and felt searing pain, like white-hot wrought
iron, tearing the calf of his leg. He passed out.

A day or so later he woke up out in some field. He had
been given a large dose of reds to knock him out. He
discovered cloth rags in the hole in his leg; essentially the
muscles of his calf had been blown out. The blood had
dried, and the pain was excruciating as he pulled the rags
out. He knew that he could not go to a hospital because
the FBI had a warrant out for him. Nor could he go home,
because his parents, whom he had wanted to kill, would

call the FBI. Besides, the chief of the Anaheim police had told them to write him off.

Incredibly Steve had only one place to turn, the same house where he was shot. Several gang members took him to the home of a nurse he knew, a neighbor of his parents. To silence her, he threatened to kill her. She cleaned out the scabs and dried blood. By the third visit to her, she finally got the courage to call Steve's parents. Steve's mother called the FBI while he was still getting his leg cleaned. When Steve and several members of the gang pulled away from the house in their car, they sensed something was up.

Steve describes what looked like a hopeless predicament:

"They used my parents' house as a stakeout. I hadn't been home in years. As we headed out of the nurse's house, I noticed this red Mustang make a U-turn. For once we weren't armed and we had no dope. Three guys were in the front seat. The pursuit began.

"As I slowed down for a red light, the Mustang ran into my rear, sending us careening into the middle of the intersection where three other cop cars suddenly wedged into us. They surrounded us with rifles and shotguns and said that if we moved, they would kill us. They pulled me out and they kicked my leg till blood really started gushing out. Then they slammed my face against the hood of my car, which in the hundred-degree summer heat caused scorching pain. Then they handcuffed my ankles and my hands together; then they handcuffed my hands to my ankles and threw me in the back of the car.

"The FBI came and looked at my leg and realized that though they had me for draft evasion, they did not have me for shooting an old lady I had been accused of shooting in attempted murder. The old lady had returned fire with a twenty-two rifle, and she hit the suspect with a twenty-two caliber bullet, and I was clearly shot by a thirty-eight bullet. This is where I saw God's hand beginning to move: The FBI let me go! And I never understood why they released me.

"But by the time I went back to the house, the gang members knew that I must have narc'd on them because I was released before they were. So I was out in the cold. That was when I started sleeping in the gutters. And I stayed so paranoid that I imagined the FBI was out to get me. And I still had to hide out from whoever it was that had the contract out on my life. So I continued living as an outlaw."

MANSION MESSIAH SOUNDS GOOD

"I was sleeping in the gutter one day and a couple, Shirley and Henry, came out to their car, which was parked near me as I lay in the gutter. They picked me up and took me inside their house, gave me a shower, fed me. She told me she saw Jesus in my eyes. Then she called three different organizations and one of those was the Mansion Messiah House of Calvary Chapel. She asked which one I would like to go to. I replied, 'I don't know, Mansion Messiah sounds good.'

"They took me over to Mansion Messiah. I walked in with my gun stuck in the back of my pants. Immediately, this little squirt named Orville looked right in my eyes and said, 'Do you know Jesus?' And I said no. And then he said, 'Bow your head, we're going to ask Jesus into your heart.' And I said the sinner's prayer after him. That happened without anyone explaining the Gospel to me.

"Everything suddenly clicked. God just grabbed my heart, reached in and burned in my heart. It was the most incredible power I have ever experienced in my life. It was a tremendous burning sensation of an inner witness. It was something of the awesomeness of God's love. I can't even express it.

"At that moment God delivered me from drugs. I flushed ten thousand dollars' worth of drugs down the toilet that day. I have never touched any drugs since that time. I also threw my gun away in the ocean. The residents of Mansion Messiah buried my clothes, they smelled so bad. From then on, I started singing Christian songs by myself when I was just walking down the street.

"For the first time in years, I telephoned my mom that same day and told her that I had accepted Jesus Christ. As I was describing what had happened to me, she got down on her knees and said, 'Anything that can save you, I want it right now.' She came to the Lord over the phone. Then I witnessed to my dad and he said, 'I don't want to hear about it. I want to see it.' So for the next seventeen years, I never witnessed to him, I just lived a changed life. But when it looked like he was dying in the hospital of cancer, I told him I could no longer hold back from discussing Christ with him. That eternity was at stake. It was then, finally, that he accepted the Lord. Since then he has survived the operation and lives on as a Christian. Those long years that my parents and I never had a relationship have been replaced by a healed relationship that we share together. In all these changes surrounding my life, I am not sure what is the greater miracle. Even my brother, Gary, came to know the Lord along with his wife, Judy."

Steve Mays comments in conclusion:

"It became a family joke when an aunt of mine, who was a Christian, would remind my parents of a prophecy about my life during some of my worst high school years. She said flatly that one day I would be a preacher. Now the impossible has happened. Not only am I, Steve Mays, a Christian, but I am a pastor as well. And who would have ever dreamed, during my most demonic years, that one day I would be pastoring a church that my own parents and brother would attend!"

CROSSING THE DESERT TO THE OASIS

But this blossoming ministry of Steve's did not happen overnight. In fact, more than once, it looked as though Steve would never even pastor a church.

In 1971 he became a resident of Mansion Messiah for a year, then switched over to another communal house for another year. It was then that Steve felt God's voice clearly tell him that he had been called to the ministry. But he had years of cobwebs to clear out of his head from drugs and general rebellion. Christian character had to be formed in Steve the slow and costly way. There is no shortcut to this.

Steve's first position that involved the responsibility of spiritual leadership came after he had spent over two years in two of our Costa Mesa houses. One day Steve felt led to go out to the California desert area of Victorville and start a Christian commune. He called my brother Paul and soon learned that they had been praying for someone to come out and start a commune.

Steve's desire was granted. Before too long, a house in Victorville was started and it had a total of thirty residents. Four Calvary Chapel pastors came out of its ministry. Steve also started a coffeehouse. Around this time, Steve started calling me weekly to bug me about giving him the go-ahead to start a church. But I did not feel he was ready. Indeed, when I finally did call him to come back to meet me one day in Costa Mesa, and he was sitting there fully expecting me to ask him to come on staff, Steve was crushed when I advised him to start a gardening business. He left to return to the Victorville commune devastated. In fact, as he said later, he felt that after all his years of reckless abandon and sin, the only plan God had in store for his life was to punish him out on the desert. And, indeed, that was where he was living at the time, in the midst of his own desert experience.

But those desert years were very important in the Spirit's preparation of Steve for the ministry that God had in mind for him. Steve had a set of my commentary tapes on the whole Bible and he began to listen to several of them each day. These tapes triggered his desire to know the Bible. His thirst for God's Word became almost insatiable and he began to build his own library of Bible commentaries which has today become one of the most extensive of any minister I know. In the desert Steve began to discover his inner spirit being satisfied by the Living Water.

Then, soon after the return to Victorville, an amazing thing happened. A pretty blonde named Gail Kroll showed up for a brief stay one day, then returned home. Immediately Steve was positive he felt God indicating to him, *There is your wife.* To double-check, he threw open the Bible and he there read a Psalm stating, "He who finds a wife finds a good thing."

He still was dubious, so Steve put God to the test. He said, "Okay, Lord, if I phone her and it just happens to be her birthday, and not only that but that no one is celebrating it with her, and in fact, she is weeping over this over the phone, then I will believe." Steve phoned her and that was exactly what the situation was. He told her over the phone, "Why don't you come out to Victorville and I will celebrate it with you." Gail left immediately. When they were having a meal that evening, Steve was too nervous to eat. Gail thought Steve was going to invite her to stay in the Victorville commune. But instead he proposed to her. To his shock, she accepted with barely a moment's thought. In a week, Steve and Gail were married and my brother performed the ceremony.

Not long after that I called Steve to his first church—on the desert. My son had started a church at 29 Palms and had moved on to Yuba City to start a ministry there. This was the last place Steve wanted to go. But he showed up, ponytail and all, to the desert community of a military base. Two years later, absolutely broken, he and Gail showed up at the Calvary Chapel Costa Mesa parking lot to find me. In silence, Steve dropped the keys of the church into my palm. The church had divided and finally closed. Steve thought that this was it, as far as the pastorate went for his life.

I immediately offered Steve the directorship of half of our Costa Mesa communal houses, including the House of Psalms, where he and Gail lived for seven years. Gail was heartbroken, because she was leaving a three-bedroom house to share a cramped house with forty other people. Their new kitchen became the meeting hall, so Gail did her dishwashing in the bathtub. But they also saw over a thousand changed lives pass through those communal houses. It was a sacrifice that had eternal rewards.

After those seven years Steve started a church in Buena Park, now known as Calvary Chapel of Cypress, then after two years was told by the Lord to leave and submit to another pastor. So for two years he was an assistant pastor at Hosannah Calvary Chapel of Belflower. He had somehow lost his priorities, he felt, and was now "remarrying the Lord." But he was also afraid that he just wasn't material to be a senior pastor. He had tried this twice and failed. But God was not finished with Steve yet. And the Lord communicated this to Steve in a beautiful and unique way, then backed it up circumstantially.

Steve had reached a point of despair in which he had finally given up ever having a church of his own. His final stipulation to the Lord was: "Chuck Smith is going to have to call me to the position." Then he went on a long-overdue vacation.

As Steve was fishing, he started talking to the Lord and asking for some kind of sign: "If I am ever going to pastor again, Lord, I am going to have to catch a fish before this hook leaves the water." Steve started to reel his line in while the hook glinted under the surface. Just as the hook was about to break through the top of the water, Steve's eyes welled up with tears. No fish would bite it now, it was too late. Just as it was coming out of the water a tiny fish bit the hook. That tiny fish meant more to Steve than any five-pound bass. For Steve detected the voice of God speaking to his soul, confirming his request for a sign, and then saying, *In a little moment, I will speak to you again.*

When Steve returned from his vacation, he got the message that he was to call me or Don McClure. He was told over the phone that there had been a meeting of all the senior pastors at the pastors' conference and that when the newly available position of pastor of the South Bay Calvary Chapel was discussed, his name was unanimously recommended. Steve was so excited he almost passed out.

Steve Mays got his church, and the board of senior pastors and I were the ones to recommend it. In 1980 he walked onto the premises of his new church. And Steve got more confirmation from the Lord. Suddenly in the sky he saw a Goodyear blimp. He heard the Lord say to him, *It's going to be a good year.*

Then Steve told the Lord that the entire board of elders would have to resign so he could start from scratch. That is exactly what happened.

In 1980 South Bay Calvary Chapel numbered 110 and occupied 1,500 square feet. Within a few years they moved to a bigger facility nearby, 15,000 square feet that they remodeled for 300,000 dollars, which is now debt-free. By then the Goodyear people had heard the often-told story of Steve's glimpsing the Goodyear blimp, so they took him up for a free ride.

It was not only a good year, but they have all been good years. The glorious harvest has come upon Steve Mays' ministry, and that church of only 110 per Sunday has grown to over 1,500.

Meanwhile the years that the powers of hell stole from Steve have been restored in a stunning way. The former dropout and quitter, as his high school coach once called him, was recently the key speaker at the Anaheim Sports Banquet. Steve's old coach gave him his letterman's jacket after seventeen years, and Steve addressed the entire football team about not giving up. Steve, who once loved baseball and who had a batting average of .450 in high school, got the chance recently to talk to the Los Angeles Dodgers, addressing the team in Dodger Stadium thanks to an invitation from his friend John Weirhaus and Victory Ministry.

Steve and Gail have two healthy children, blue-eyed blondes who don't have any sign of Steve's scars. They excel in sports, academics, and loving obedience. And Gail has a home she can be proud of, much nicer than the one she had to abandon at 29 Palms, plus her own cattery in which she raises Himalayan cats.

Steve now sees that God has flooded his life with almost more grace than he can contain. He is a living testimony. To use his own words, "By the grace of God, I have not only regained what Satan ripped off, but I have been given a greater abundance of positive effects than all the evil I heaped up in the past."

We have seen a life literally go from the gutter to grace. The only thing Steve carries on his body to remind him of his former years is that painful scar on his leg. To this day, it still hurts. It serves as a reminder to teach Steve gratitude, to never forget the pit from which he came, and the greatness of God's grace that brought him out of that pit.

Zechariah speaks of the days when Zerubbabel had laid the foundations for the rebuilding of the new Temple and that there were those who despised the days of small things. Steve, for a time, was caught in that desire to build the walls before the foundation was laid. In this he learned that it is vitally important not to build out of sequence, but to dig deep and lay the foundation on the Rock.

6

Jon Courson: Fire & Rain Descend on Applegate Valley

 Jon Courson stood on the banks of Yale Creek in the Applegate Valley of Oregon. This husky fellow was silhouetted against the vibrant green all around him, as his thick mane of red hair shone in the summer sun. Before him stood the members of a colony of young people who had built a treehouse community in the Applegate hills. They were standing in the nude in the middle of the river waiting to be baptized and resembled aging nature children as their long hair blew and glinted in the sunshine.

Jon felt conflict over whether or not to make an issue over their nudity. He went with his gut sense, and decided to overlook it. This group before him had for years been a community of pot-growers whose treehouse community was on a large tract of land they owned. Their marijuana harvests had made large proceeds for them while their "Nirvana Community" had looked for enlightenment through Eastern yoga and native American shamanism. But the bubble of their dream had burst. Just when they had built their ideal community, a gaping vacuum appeared within their hearts. This huge utopian experiment had not satisfied their souls.

Then in the late seventies Jon Courson appeared in their wilderness community with his wife, Terry. Soon, gently, this broad-shouldered Christian neighbor of theirs started to tell the treehouse-dwellers about the love of Christ as he joined them in the stream over the months. He would run his hands through the water and talk about his faith. They saw a strength and a hope shining in his eyes, a joy, that they had not found. Jon seemed to have no need for drugs or any other kicks. He was as solid to them as a California redwood. But his strength did not come from himself, but from the One whom he continually told them about.

With waves of mounting inner joy, Jon baptized each one of them in the name of Christ. They stood on the banks dripping and smiling ear to ear. That evening they would gather up all their marijuana and burn it up in a huge bonfire.

Jon, meanwhile, was overseeing a church being built from scratch in a region of Oregon so sparsely populated that no demographically oriented church planner would ever try what Jon was attempting. Applegate was a region containing verdant mountains, forests, and clear rivers with a widespread population of fewer than a thousand.

It was near the northern California border, and from there to Eureka, California, tribes of pot-growers tilled their crops, some of them with semi-automatic rifles. The leader of this community, once notorious, was now giving up his rich lifestyle to follow Christ.

This was the first of five waves of pot-growing converts in the Applegate Valley. This particular group became tree-planters in their Oregon community. One of their members eventually became the pastor of a Calvary Chapel church in the state of Washington. Another became a pastor under Jon.

Recently I got a letter from a spin-off fellowship from Jon's church in Ashland, Oregon, that now has 600 members. The letter described the impact from a major commune of pot-growers who had become Christians. What had happened was this. A few of them went to the Ashland Calvary Fellowship where they got some of my Bible-teaching tapes, and began to play them while they worked on their marijuana harvests. One day they asked themselves, "Is what we are doing right?" Soon after that they accepted Christ en masse, burned their pot, joined the fellowship, and started a natural food business called Maranatha Nuts that made various kinds of nut butters and natural foods. Theirs has become the most successful business in the region. When I read their letter in Calvary Chapel Costa Mesa, there was extended applause.

When Jon first came to Oregon, he had only five couples attending his fellowship. He had left a thriving Calvary Chapel that he and his brother had started in San Jose. But he was certain the hand of God was directing his move.

Before Jon moved to Oregon, during a teaching retreat with the Christian couples, there were two prophetic visions about the coming harvest. The first vision was of fire descending on Applegate Valley and then spreading beyond. The second vision of massive thunderheads pouring out rain foresaw the end of Oregon's long drought. And a further message in this was that God's grace would be released when the first rains came. Jon was reluctant to accept these visions as prophecies and was by no means sure he would leave San Jose for Oregon. Interestingly, the day Jon began his first Sunday service there, the rains came flooding down. He also sensed in his heart that God's grace was being released.

Today Applegate, Oregon, is still a community of only a thousand people. But its Calvary Chapel fellowship, Applegate Christian Fellowship, is known throughout the region. Its church membership is actually three times the size of the town's population—three thousand members— all coming in from surrounding communities. They are now meeting in a large church facility of 40,000 square feet that they built together. Vast beams run along the ceiling and huge plate-glass windows look out into the beautiful valley. In the summer, they meet in a large grass-covered outdoor amphitheater near the main church building. Both structures and a vast parking lot sit on their forty acres. The outdoor amphitheater is bordered by flowers and surrounded by an excellent sound system. It can seat over 2,000. I had the pleasure of dedicating the new church building recently and large pictures of the event headlined local papers.

Jon has experienced the fire and the rain of this harvest. He will tell you flatly that it is a miracle. Indeed, fourteen other spin-off Calvary Chapels have come out of this one enormous church. John Peterson went to Grants Pass initially while Guy Gray went to Medford. Soon others followed. They had witnessed the huge crowds assembling in Cantrel Buckley Park to hear Jon preach in the summer and fall months of 1978 and 1979. Jon is often reminded of that early vision of fire descending on Applegate Valley and spreading outward to other communities.

Jon has also learned that there is a purifying aspect to

fire in biblical imagery in which one's work for God is tested in the fire. And all hay and stubble is burned leaving only the enduring works of gold and precious gems. Jon has also experienced these waves of fire, at times of testing, and has seen his church rebuilt on stronger foundations following each wave.

PIONEERING INTO NEW TERRITORIES

A little more than ten years ago, Calvary Chapel fellowships and churches started spreading out beyond California and opening up in various parts of the country. Those who pioneered these churches, like Jon Courson, almost without exception spent time at Costa Mesa learning and fellowshiping with us. At the right time each would feel the nudge from God and move out. As can happen, there are some who are not of our fellowship who have used our name for their own ends. Now and then we hear reports of wild activities that in no way reflect our fellowship. We believe in the church-building approach that only humility and the love of Christ can bring, not modern extravaganzas or money collection schemes.

Calvary Chapel pioneers came from a diverse range of backgrounds. Jon Courson was a student at Biola College in nearby La Mirada, Los Angeles, when he started attending Calvary Chapel. Unlike some of our ministers with more sensational and bizarre backgrounds, Jon represented the epitome of normalcy, adjustment, and graceful conformity. He stood out as America's ideal son of moral virtue and hard work when contrasted with some of the wild rebels among us. And without a doubt, Jon has added a significant piece to the mosaic that God is building through Calvary Chapel's ministries. The picture would be incomplete without his "type." For he further adds to the design that God uses all people to serve him: from the outrageous, like Steve Mays and Mike MacIntosh, to those like himself and George Markey who represent the unscathed center of the American heartland.

Jon Courson and George Markey, a big strapping mid-Western farm boy who pioneered a Calvary Chapel in his rural farm community (now with 1,000 members), could probably walk comfortably into early America. They are our nation's Johnny Appleseeds and Paul Bunyans—the carryovers from former eras of national innocence and purity compared to present-day sophistication. They are products of old American virtues, a fact that can be evidenced on their beaming faces—handsome faces radiating virile strength tempered by gentle self-control. I am afraid they are a vanishing breed of men. Replacing them is what some call "the new male."

And this brings me to a subject that greatly burdens me. Permit me, if you will, to digress for a moment over an issue that is critical to our time. Our world and its media have turned against the old traditional order of men and women and all that they stand for, as it applauds the new androgynous male and female roles.

The new male has shunned what for time immemorial has been recognized as healthy masculinity for a new "liberated" blending of added feminine traits. This is nothing new. It is the scale on which this transition is happening that bothers me. As someone said, they have become "women-thinking men," or "touchy/feely men" and they are anything but equipped to head a household or sire a healthy family. Rather, they herald the age of single-parent families and confused sex role models as they sport the latest markings of their newfound freedoms. They are men who wear single earrings, fellows with unisex haircuts who have brazenly strayed into the women's side of the department store. And they have done it with defiant pride, encouraged by sneering anti-male women who themselves have trampled underfoot any wholesome femininity that they might have had for a brash, defiant, pseudo-masculine hardness.

Meanwhile the new touchy/feely men have joined the shrill voices in protest against any reminder of the once-common strong traditional male. This gale of voices can be heard on almost any college campus, headed by the lesbian and feminist coalitions and assorted anti-traditional and leftist minorities and causes. They would put traditional America, and all historical records of it, through the shredder if they could. The New World Order they espouse is collectivist, amoral, anti-family, anti-American, and anti-Christian. The ideal of a biblical man who is strong and not vacillating or weak is anathema to them. An intimidated "wimp" is far less threatening.

This group postures as broad-minded and nonjudgmental—and so they are as long as you happen to be "gay," feminist, liberal, liberationist, socialist, or Marxist. But if you are a Christian, especially a "traditional" white male, then you are targeted. And they can employ the full sanction of "enlightened" society to hurl any judgments at you they wish with total impunity. The uncommitted middle-of-the-roaders, who are fearful of being singled out, will contort wildly to avoid having any loaded accusations hurled at them; terms like "sexist" and "racist" will bring all sorts of people into line. A football player and a college professor will wilt before a group of wild-eyed feminists that has labeled them "sexist." Indeed, intimidated people have given this ugly and bent coalition unilateral power to judge and define them at whim.

An agenda of social castration has almost been fully consummated, and the results are sordid. It is like the king with no clothes: A college president will perform delicate pirouettes to avoid speaking in non-inclusive language at commencement exercises so he won't offend various feminists and minorities present. The word "person" is suddenly affixed to every other word. It is a perfect instance of what Orwell called double-think. And few have the courage to stand against this ugly trend headed by a shrill-voiced minority who would have barely spoken above a whisper forty years ago.

In all of this, the atmosphere between the sexes has become contentious, cynical, and mistrusting. Individual "rights" are so on the forefront that the bonding of men and women in marriage is close to an impossibility. And divorce statistics bear this out.

Have you noticed that men and women are hardly falling in love anymore? This causes the homosexual groups to gloat privately. In today's atmosphere it is little wonder that this is so when you consider that modern society resembles what Paul describes in his second letter to Timothy: The social rebellion has truly been incredible.

Jon Courson felt called by God to stand against the beginnings of this social rebellion by being a role model. At the time, the latest anarchy was the hippie movement of the late '60s.

A NORMAL APPLE PIE YOUTH

Jon had fully distinguished himself as an outstanding athlete and scholar by the time he was in high school. He was senior class president and captain of the football team. By the time of his graduation, his class honored him with three awards, an unprecedented action: He was voted most popular, best personality, and best outlook on life. He was also winner of the Principal's Cup as the outstanding senior graduate of his high school. Finally, Jon won the District Superintendent's Cup as the outstanding senior graduate for his whole district in Northern California.

As President of the Baptist Youth of Northern California, Jon already had an active speaking ministry during high school. He addressed youth retreats, camps, and church groups. As a hero figure, Jon's life proclaimed the virtue of godly obedient living over and above the rebellion so glamorized by America's youth. Here was a healthy and handsome honor society student who was a football captain who managed to have fun and fulfillment without having to resort to drugs and corrupting influences. He was saying, "You don't have to be a rebel to be fulfilled or happy."

Consistent with Jon's disciplined life, he received a full athletic scholarship to Biola University, a Christian school. He held the discus record of both his high school and its conference league. By the time that this broad-shouldered big-armed young man was hurling the discus in college, he ranked eighth nationally in the NAIA college division. He had also begun riding his ten-speed bicycle out to Calvary Chapel on weekends and spending Saturday nights on the bathroom floor. This we learned later.

Jon's zeal was undoubtedly hard to miss. Yet there were things happening inside him that would direct his life on an unexpected course. Jon's well-calculated path of conformity and honorable good deeds had some problems.

He was a popular man on campus who bathed in all the outward rewards of being a do-gooder and role model. He was the cream of the crop of Baptist youth and fully expected to walk into a well-appointed ministry. The mechanism was all set in motion.

The problem was that this young zealot was beginning to be confronted with issues that required hard and costly decisions. He was also having an intense new encounter with God. And that can be dangerous and costly to one's plans, designs, and ambitions. Among other things, none of us can appreciate God's grace until we realize how greatly our "good" actions fall short of the perfection and goodness of God's standards. Our greatest efforts are cheap imitations.

Jon was also working through some theological questions. Back then, some of Jon's professors were suspicious of Calvary Chapel and delivered subtle warnings that we should be avoided. There was a little too much going on out here as far as they were concerned. Besides, that could signal cultish activity.

Jon, however, was not persuaded by his professors. He felt instead that God was being kept in a box by the academic theologizing of history. He also felt the constraints of spiritual legalism: A tight and regimented system of piety quenched him. He felt he was participating "in a form of godliness but denying the power thereof," as the Scripture itself warns. He felt trapped and hemmed in by a system that discouraged encounters with God of the sort reported in the Bible. Jon was studying the vitality of the early Church in the book of Acts, with its sense of reality and mission and power, and wondered why modern Christianity had to settle for a diminished and powerless faith. Had God changed through history? Had He mellowed into deism? The powerful early Church was relegated to ancient history. It stood before Jon teasingly, as if he were watching a banquet in an exclusive club through a window.

Jon came to Calvary Chapel in the fall of 1972. He has often shared his initial reaction. "All of a sudden I was gripped with this incredible certainty that all that I had been studying in the classroom about the book of Acts was happening before my very eyes. That it was suddenly real and was truly happening today. I was astonished over the possibility that I could find New Testament reality today. That it can be a reality now. It revolutionized my life. The spiritual dryness inside of me suddenly flooded with restored hope and vitality."

Unlike most of our Calvary Chapel pastors, Jon grew up in a strong Christian home. But he had to battle things that his peers were unaware of, namely, that unending seduction of good works and legalism that can stand in the path of so many Christians. It can make you lose sight of the miracle of God's grace so easily, and cause you to follow tight rules while judging all other believers ungraciously in the process. This legalistic trap vexes Christians time and again. They end up spiritually paralyzed, joyless, and without love. Certainly without the love of God Jon could not have seen those waves of conversions in Applegate Valley.

A key moment of reckoning for Jon came when he was addressing hundreds of youth. All of a sudden God pointed to Jon's heart and said, *You don't care about these kids at all. You are expounding truth with absolutely no love for them. You have no love for them at all. And that is a lie.* For two days after that Jon drove around in his surfing van. He told God that if he was not given love to minister with, he would abandon his plans of going into the ministry.

By Jon's graduation, he had told the Baptist conference that he wanted to work with Calvery Chapel. Immediately, their doors of opportunity slammed in his face. Calvary was still very much an emerging and misunderstood ministry. "Non-denominational" can be a term that denominational churches become suspicious of. After Jon's graduation, he taught for a year at our Twin Peaks conference center in the mountains above San Bernardino. And a year or so after that, after he and his brother had started the church in San Jose, he and his wife, Terry, were off to Oregon. But a vicious trial lay ahead of this stouthearted fellow of which he would have no clue.

TRIALS BY FIRE

Until a few years ago Jon could have been accused of having it easy. He did not come from a family of five stepfathers like Greg Laurie, or a family that was coolly rejecting, like Steve Mays. Jon Courson's family was the embodiment of American wholesomeness. He was loved and cherished by his parents. His mother was such an intercessor, she literally used to weep into the pages of her Bible when she prayed and read Scripture. A home such as this today is a statistical rarity. Jon's testimony had been, "If you follow the Lord, He will bless you as He has me. You don't need to be a rebel." Jon could trace the moment of his salvation to the young age of three-and-a-half, when he consciously gave his life to Christ during an evangelistic rally that his parents had gone to with Jon in their arms. Jon remembers that moment as clearly as if it had been yesterday.

Yet, in the lives of even the best of Christians there are hard times, times of testing and times of drought. There are times that fire will consume some part of our lives to reveal what lies hidden. It is never easy. There are unexpected tragedies that come along and sift our souls in ways we never thought possible. And that is what happened to Jon. For one day, in one moment, the beautiful wife of his youth, Terry, was taken from him. It happened on a country road in Oregon, the winter of 1982, as Jon and Terry were driving down Highway 42 to Mount Bachelor. In an instant, his car slid on a sheet of ice, spun around, and slammed into a tree.

As he was crawling along the road looking for help he knew in his heart that Terry was dead. In the ambulance, the Holy Spirit spoke the words from Jeremiah 29:11 to him as it sped toward the town of Medford. The verse hung soberly in Jon's mind: *I know the thoughts that I think toward you. They are of peace and goodness and not of evil to bring you to a certain end.* Jon questioned why God had taken Terry, but never with bitterness, anger, or doubt toward God. He was on an emotional roller-coaster. Yet beneath it he felt a peace that passes all understanding. God had assured him: *Jon, I have promised and given you a peace that passes all understanding. So do not seek a peace that comes from understanding. It does not work that way.*

Three years later, God gave Jon a beautiful wife named Tammy who has borne him two more children. She is lithe and young and loves him to pieces. Jon has learned that what Satan means for evil, God will turn for good through mercy and grace.

And that is the message of Jon's life and ministry. "As for me, I'm called to love. Our emphasis is on love." And many, in that expanding group of fellowships, have had vital encounters with the eternal love of Christ. There have been fire and rain in Applegate Valley and Jon has been blessed by being God's instrument in this.

Jon's life shows us that God is by no means limited to using converted rebels or people with heavy testimonies. Look at all of the Bible figures God used who came out of godly backgrounds. God can and will use any person who surrenders to Him. The only question is the willingness on the part of the individual.

Christ speaks of a banquet to which the aristocrats were invited. When they turned down the invitation, it became a beggars banquet. They were the only ones needy enough to come. The rest were out there "making it" in the world. It is a rare thing for someone who "has it all" not to be tempted by worldly admiration and accolades, peer pressure and money, and the pleasures of life. It all comes too easily. That is why so few who do "have it all" are willing to sacrifice it all for the sake of the Kingdom of God. When they do, the results can be impressive as God uses them in His work.

7

Raul Ries: Hope Ripples from Out of the Shaft of Oblivion

Raul Ries, as a youth and as a young man, was a Latin street fighter from South of the border. He crossed the Mexican border as a boy to escape his crazed alcoholic father. But Los Angeles was no rose garden for him either. By his early twenties Raul was a case-hardened Marine veteran out of Vietnam, a kung fu expert, and still the perennial street fighter. By then he was testy, suspicious, and full of rage. He used to jump at people like a Doberman pinscher: He would back someone against a wall, almost snarling, freezing them with fear. Should the quarry move or fight back, Raul would tear him apart.

How could a man come to have this much anger and hatred? Surely it started with the cruelty he and his family suffered at the hands of his alcoholic father. Perhaps it grew in the frustration of church rituals he didn't understand. It was probably fed by the fact that, physically, Raul was incredibly powerful, quick, and had the kind of stamina that could go all night. Attacking others was one way he could fight back. By the time he was in high school, Raul was the leader of a fierce L.A. street gang. His reputation around West Covina, the Latin Quarter of Los Angeles, made him someone to be feared. Finally after an assault and battery charge for crippling a football player on an opposing high school team at a party, the judge suggested that if Raul liked to fight so much, he should join the Marines, otherwise he might be looking at some time in jail. Raul opted for the Marines and went on a tour of duty in Vietnam. It was there that he killed again and again, winning the Purple Heart medal in the process. He also got something else, on the inside of his soul.

Something happens to you when you kill another man. A primal nerve is cut and a kind of innocence is lost. No one, who hasn't gone through this, can fully understand it. The imagination can't fill in for the lack of experience. It is the dilemma of those Civil War soldiers in *Red Badge of Courage*. They could never guess what their reactions were going to be before their first real confrontation with battle; and usually they were utterly surprised to find out how they behaved and thought. It was almost as if they were strangers to a hidden part of themselves. Then, after killing, they suddenly gained a terrible self-knowledge. Joseph Conrad, with stunning artistry, was able to reveal this shadow-self in his classic work *Heart of Darkness*.

Raul, too, encountered his own heart of darkness in the jungles of Vietnam. It was there that he encountered his shadow side. It helped him survive in an alien and primitive world, far from the civilized West. The shadow-self had its uses. But its jungle strengths stood in stark contrast to those gentler values of the free world. And once in the free world again, this shadowy nature could still come uncoiling out, like some sort of Oriental demon.

A Jekyll and Hyde incident would take place at one time or another, and it would invariably terrify those helpless onlookers who had never encountered this magnitude of violence. In the end, it was this homicidal, darker side that brought Raul to the brink of extinction. He planned one final killing rampage that almost worked.

This time his victims were not Vietcong, but the helpless and alienated members of his own family. His life had gone 'way out of control and his wife and children were terrified of him. He was abusing them more and more while his inflamed appetites drew him to other women.

This particular night his wife had gone to church with the kids. And when Raul discovered their packed suitcases, he knew they planned to leave him.

Raul burned with a bitter and jealous rage. Rather than have his family walk out on him—and eventually take up with another man—Raul decided to do what we see in the headlines more and more these days: If they could not live together, then they would all die together. Like the ancient Egyptians in Thebes and Karnak, Raul planned to board his family on the boat of Anubis into the abyss. But this thought flavored his rage with unspeakable remorse.

There was no escape from the fact that the only people on earth that Raul had ever loved would be dead. And this would be a final seal of ultimate and absolute failure upon his soul. This sadness drifted in and out of his thoughts like a painful breeze.

Raul sat, paced, or crouched on the floor of his living room with a loaded rifle, waiting. If the door moved, he would explode into action like a panther. That was the plan. Just take them out as quickly as possible. Then he would turn the gun on himself.

But time stretched on and on. So to placate this inner

hell, Raul resorted to turning on the TV. He flipped the channels around till he froze the channel selector on my face. I was holding the Sunday evening service at Calvary Chapel Costa Mesa. Apparently I was less grating on his nerves than the other programs. But, in time, the message that I was sharing began to sink into Raul's soul.

Raul has described that desperate moment many times, and written about it in his book, *From Fury to Freedom.*

Gradually Raul began listening to the words he was hearing.

I was teaching about the love of God—a love so great that He was willing to give His beloved Son in the place of us sinners. Raul began to think about this. God couldn't really care about him that much, not about someone so evil. That kind of love couldn't be free for the asking . . . or could it? He kept listening.

"You see, God is perfect," I was saying. "And in His holiness, He can't have anything to do with us sinners. But He loves us so much that He Himself took the just penalty for all the sins in all of our lives."

No! This is too good to believe.

"God wants you to know that in spite of what you may be or in spite of what you may have done—you may have messed up your life completely—God still loves you. He is reaching out to you and inviting you to come and to share that love with Him, no matter how deeply you may have gone into sin. Jesus offers forgiveness to us as a free gift. All we have to do is accept it."

Raul's heart pounded. Without realizing it he put the gun down. The longing for forgiveness overwhelmed him. He was beginning to believe what he was hearing. He slipped off the chair and onto his knees in front of the

TV screen. When I gave the invitation to pray, Raul responded, his body rocking with heavy sobs.

After he prayed he decided to drive as fast as he could to the church that was televising the service. He wanted to make a public confession.

Soon he was standing in the back of that huge church and almost ran down to the front when those who wanted to give their lives to Christ were asked to come forward.

It was the same church that his wife and kids had gone to earlier.

This was the turning point for Raul Ries. And God, and not I, was the divine agent in this miracle, make no mistake about it. I am just glad that I had some role in it as a participant. And I have been overjoyed to see what has been happening with Raul Ries ever since that critical moment. He and his family could have died that night. Instead they are a happy and normal family and Raul has a huge ministry. I ask myself, can raising the dead be that much more incredible a miracle?

Today Raul Ries looks so completely different that it is almost impossible to associate his dark past with the same man. Looking at Raul Ries you see a man who could easily pass for a professor of Latin studies at an Ivy League university. His Castilian face, outlined in clear-rim glasses, his neatly trimmed hair, pin-striped shirt, and necktie, give him the dignified and sober appearance of an academic. This, added to his look of humble, keen-witted intelligence, makes his past seem totally implausible.

An air of kindness, virtue, peace, and contentment emanates from Raul. His constant smile and loving countenance totally belie the fierce hatred that once boiled inside. There seems to be only one way to account for this: either a major miracle has occurred, or we are dealing with a completely different man. But we knew he is the same man. The one thing that has remained unchanged has been Raul's associations: Raul still has the same wife, kids, parents, and associates who knew him in the old days. He also has the same fingerprints. Like the congenitally blind man who stood before Christ, his testimony to unbelieving opponents is powerfully simple: "Wherefore I was once blind, now I see." And nobody who has known the man can argue with this. It stands in history.

So great was Raul's change that those who knew him had to pinch themselves to make sure that it was not all a dream. And almost all of the people who witnessed Raul's alarming change are themselves changed because of it. They have become Christians and most of them attend Raul's church.

And that brings us to another amazing fact. The radical change in Raul's life has not stopped or changed direction but it has gathered more and more positive momentum as he has influenced other lives. His life has gathered speed like a boulder rolling down a mountainside that hits some lake below, and the ripples keep going out and out.

Raul is now the pastor of a church that he planted ten years ago. It has grown from a Bible study of thirty in a single room—his old kung fu studio—to a massive Calvary Chapel of over five thousand! And it stands right at the footstep of the old neighborhood that he used to terrorize, West Covina, Los Angeles. The ripple effect continues.

Raul has gone on numerous evangelistic missions, not only into the heart of Los Angeles, but into the heart of Mexico and Latin America, where he has spoken to thousands. He is also on the airwaves daily in California and other areas of the country on a popular radio show. And I am convinced that one day in heaven, we will see a long line of his greater Latin family extending out as far as the eye can see. And this will be due, in no small part, to the ripple effect of Raul's life.

There seems to be a pattern in Calvary Chapel that those from various backgrounds are used in a kind of divine symmetry in relation to their past and their abilities. If they have reaped certain kinds of ill effects in the past, often they return to these areas and have a reverse effect that more than makes up for all the negative ripples that they created initially. This is a byproduct of grace, and not the efforts of these men striving to make up for all the bad they have done. It is a fruit of their lives, not a plan outlined in some tactical administrative session. It is one of those deeper redemptive patterns of God by no means unique to Calvary Chapel. We see this redemptive sym-metry time and again, a kind of awe-inspiring economy of effort.

Raul's ministry powerfully reflects this divine economy. His communicative gifts and his background are tailor-made for a cross-section of people who need to be reached and can best be reached by his unique approach. I am referring to the millions of Latins from L.A., Mexico, Chile, Central America, and beyond, who have only the most fragmented idea of what Christianity is all about. Most of the time, they know a few token rituals that they have half-heartedly performed. They have an outsider's serf relationship to a big sprawling religious entity, the Church of Rome, that they barely comprehend. It is shrouded in mystery, and they seldom approach their priests except in moments of crisis.

A significant number of Latin people are completely alienated from the Catholic system, the way Raul had been most of his life. They virtually never have anything to do with the Church, yet the Church is still their sole model of Christianity. Frankly this image of the Church can act as a barrier to keep them from ever hearing the words of Christ. The priesthood stands forever in their minds as the sole link of mediation between ordinary men and God.

If Paul the apostle could claim to be all things to all men, at least Raul can say to his people, "I, too, was part of a church system I didn't understand. I was a man's man and a feared brawler. I had a tough childhood in Mexico City and Los Angeles. I drank, fought, killed, and had more women than I knew what to do with. I, too, had an alcoholic father, like so many of you. I, too, was abused and beaten as a child. I, too, grew up in a poor, uneducated home. And I know what it is like to feel like a second-class citizen in America. I know what that stare of racism is like. I had to face it in the Marines and in police stations." Raul, in many ways, represents the collective dilemma of the Latin people. And it is precisely this that God has used to reach these very people who are as alienated as the hippies were in their heyday. God's economy of grace is seen with rare power in the ministry of Raul Ries.

After the night Raul came forward in my church, the evidence of his changed life became plain to everyone. So was the consistency of his life. He immersed himself in the Bible, started immediately to share his faith, and began leading Bible studies at home, and listening to tapes. The Holy Spirit was his teacher, not a seminary.

But it was not always easy. Raul had to face his ghosts of the past. Before his ministry ever grew, he had to suffer adversity for his faith. For a while he was as "uncool" and unpopular as he had once been popular for all the bad things he had done. In short Raul had to pay a price for his new-found faith, and this is something that many Christians are not willing to do. They become embarrassed Christians, a silent majority that passively waits for God to raise up superstars to do it all for them.

If Raul's sprawling church is impressive now, it was not always that way. With its current success, it is easy to see why people want to emulate it or study it in graduate programs on church growth for quick, easy formulas. But Raul's approach was to throw his life into the hands of God, obediently, come good or ill. If God indicated something to Raul, and it seemed costly, he would still do it unquestioningly. You see, in a way, he had nothing to lose. He was a dead man the night of his conversion. He would have been a statistic in the newspapers. So every hard step up after that has been gratefully taken.

And they were hard steps. When he tried to share his faith at his lucrative kung fu school, people dropped away rapidly and his finances dried up. When he went to his old high school to share his faith in the school cafeteria, he ended up with mashed potato and other food on his face and clothes. But Raul persisted, sensing God's direction.

SIGNS OF RAUL'S MINISTRY

Then one day it happened—the first evidences of Raul's harvest. At lunchtime, as Raul was sharing his faith boldly with at least half of the student body, he gave a call and four hundred high schoolers came forward to accept Christ. This was one-fifth the student body of Baldwin Park High School, the very school from which Raul had been ejected and expelled numerous times.

Today most of these students, now grown up and with

families, go to Raul's church. They helped form the nucleus of the church in the early days of the church in 1975.

Then one night in his church, even the impossible happened: Raul's alcoholic father walked down the aisle to dedicate his life to Christ. This man who had been so impossible to live with, so cruel to his family, whom Raul had been an adversary of all his life, was now changed. For the child of an alcoholic, such a change represents a miraculous gift. A huge burden was lifted from Raul's shoulders, one he had been carrying all of his life.

Today Raul's church, Calvary Chapel West Covina, spills over with people during all three Sunday services. There is a feverish excitement, a sense of expectation. The impressive sanctuary is remodeled from the hollowed-out insides of a large Safeway store. The main auditorium is almost two-thirds the size of a football field. Its stage has the simple Calvary Chapel emblem, and is usually loaded with musical equipment—speakers, drums, a piano, guitar amps and keyboards. Before Raul comes out to share and teach, there is about forty minutes of worship service. Everyone joins in singing along with various solo artists or groups that happen to be playing.

Raul is alive and dynamic. His engaging style seems to pull out the individual. What he says is relevant to them. Raul usually shines with joy when he speaks. If he has slipped, the members of the church will be given the example of how it happened and how God's grace dug Raul out. Maybe he almost got into a shouting match on an L.A. freeway. But the grace of God calmed Raul down and he asked the man to forgive him. In all of this is hope, as Raul shares from his heart in utter transparency.

Clearly here is a man who is sincere and content, he is also committed to what he says and never fails to mention his Savior with reverent enthusiasm. If you talk to his people, you learn of his integrity and his purity of lifestyle. Raul is a beacon of Christian character, purity, and dedication. Sunday after Sunday this very gifted and intelligent speaker stands before them as a constant reminder of a miracle. The miracle of someone supernaturally changed from the inside out.

The Holy Spirit works through individuals. Each individual identity is preserved and becomes the medium that God uses as a microphone to communicate His truths to others. Raul remains Raul, from his idiosyncrasies of gesture, to his Mexican accent, to his slang, to his emotional outbursts of enthusiasm, to his moments of calm or sad reflection. These form the tapestry of what God has done.

Raul Ries went from oblivion to joy. I look at God's economy of purpose in awe and know that none but God could put this kind of beautiful living poem together.

8

Jeff Johnson: From Big-Time Drug Deals to Feeding Thousands the Eternal Word

Jeff Johnson needed a lot of space. He settled himself deep in the jungle of Oahu, a Hawaiian island, surrounded by thick tropical foliage, absolutely alone. Jeff had been in Hawaii for several months in his pursuit of the "clear light." Now he was going to make the ultimate leap of his life. It was late summer 1968.

Jeff fasted for four days. He had brought a minimum of necessities and lived in a tent. His plan was to drop the biggest dose of LSD-25 he had ever taken, and as a drug pusher, Jeff had taken some enormous doses. But this time, he had an occult formula to follow. Jeff would become a modern shaman and follow an ancient path. Like Carlos Castaneda's accounts of his tutelage under an Indian sorcerer, Jeff was trying to meet with the primeval powers and forces to find a higher reality.

The film *Emerald Forest* portrays a white boy growing up

deep in the interior of the jungles of Brazil. He was first kidnaped and then adopted by a tribe that had never contacted the modern outside world until bulldozers pushed deep into the Brazilian jungle. The youth learned to adopt their alternate way of thinking. He entered the shamanistic rites of the tribe at his initiation into manhood. On a powerful rare jungle plant, he experienced the ultimate psychedelic, and gained the shamanistic ability to turn into various animals. He could soar in the sky as a hawk. Or he could command the frogs to chirp, thus bringing on flood. The film is a seductive look into New Age beliefs—the psychic powers within, the inner self, oneness with nature, and mind-altering experiences. Jeff's rite in the jungle of Oahu, ten years before this film, certainly anticipated its teaching. He wanted to tap the hidden wisdom behind nature.

Before coming to the island of Oahu, Jeff had built up a considerable business pushing drugs in Southern California. He had managed to stay stoned on anything he wanted. But Jeff was also on a spiritual search. He had been pursuing the mystical teachings of Yogananda and the Self Realization Fellowship before leaving California.

Now Jeff was seeing a connection between Yogananda's teachings and the latest pronouncements of acid guru Timothy Leary, who often hung out in Hawaii. Leary's classic book, *The Psychedelic Experience*, was the method Leary advocated for finding the "clear light" by a shortcut through an ancient Tibetan Buddhistic rite. Instead of decades of yoga and astral travel and guidance through death planes, as the Tibetan Book of the Dead demanded of its adepts, Leary taught that it could now be done immediately with LSD. In fact Leary had translated this ancient Tibetan text in modern jargon and reset its rituals for LSD journeys. Acid was the modern discovery providing instant access to the wisdom of the ancients, Leary assured his surging audiences of flower children.

Jeff, until now, was living with fourteen others in a two-bedroom communal house. It bordered the jungle within the interior of the island of Oahu. But there had been problems. Half the "freaks" were on LSD, and that was fine for Jeff. But the other half were on reds, downers, and that made for some bad communication. For instance, Jeff would be in the Lotus position, upside-down, trying to get his "third eye" to open. Then someone on reds would crash through the door with all the sensitivity of a bull and ask, "Hey, man, what are you doing?"

Jeff would respond in irritation, "What do you mean, what am I doing? I'm getting in tune with God. You guys ought to clean up your act. You're taking all these downers and they're going to kill you. You ought to get where I am—in the high plane."

There were other rough edges to paradise. With everybody high and doing his own thing, nobody kept house. The dishes were stacked up to the ceiling. They were covered with mold and had started to smell. And fixing food was a major effort. Another thin edge to the dream was that most of the residents had to write home for money. They needed the straight world to keep them aloft.

So Jeff headed for isolation in the jungle. The acid that Jeff dropped there was tainted with strychnine, a rat poison. Dealers often cut LSD-25 with other chemicals, and strychnine, in smaller quantities, was a popular cut since it could act like speed. But in the quantities that Jeff took, it could be lethal. Countercultural chemistry had certainly gone beyond ethics. You did not always know what you were buying.

For two days Jeff battled for his life. He retched and vomited nonstop while staggering and holding onto plants and trees. At night he swayed back and forth in the center of the tent. He entered a topsy-turvy atavistic jungle realm. He had walked through the door of an alien universe: He could hear ants; he see and hear the bark of trees talking. Sounds came ripping through the jungle's interior that he never dreamed existed. After two days, when the strychnine effects wore off, the LSD seemed to throttle his mind with full force.

On the third day a giant horsefly came into the tent and landed on Jeff's wrist. Jeff tried to hook his will to the fly with meditative force. He told the fly to flip over, and it did. Then he had it zooming patterns in the air. Jeff seemed to be able to get the fly to do anything. After several hours he let it go, mentally, and it flew out of the tent. As Jeff remembers, "The lord of the flies, Beelzebul, gave me a small sample of power."

It had been raining for two days. Now it had cleared and the air tingled with freshness. Jeff went outside and fell asleep on the jungle floor. He had been completely naked for some time. To Jeff's horror, he woke up in the early dawn with thousands of spiders and bugs all over him.

I will let him narrate this moment in his own words:

"I started to go out of my mind. I didn't know where I was. I started to panic. Fear took hold of me and I started to run through the jungle naked. Spider webs and all kinds of brush and tree branches swept by me as I ran out of control. I was scratched and bleeding. It was a terrible nightmare. I was lost in the jungle and had no idea how to get out. I had no clothes and I was totally disoriented. I began crying convulsively, knowing that I had lost my mind. Little did I know that God had His hand on me, protecting me through this deadly episode.

"All of a sudden I fell down over a cliff and rolled onto a main dirt road that led out of the jungle. I got on that road and ended up on the edge of a cliff that overlooked the north shore of Oahu. As I stood over the cliffs of Sunset Beach and Wihamea Bay, I felt Satan's presence. I began to chant the sanskrit sound of *om*—the supposed primeval sound of the universe. My voice was getting louder and louder. As I had controlled the horsefly, I now wanted to control wider areas of nature in a godlike manner. This time I focused on the waves. Perhaps my senses were deceiving me, but I began to see it happen.

"My thoughts, as I chanted, were to bring the waves up from the sea to devour everybody who was down there. The waves were coming and I could see the swells getting bigger. Soon the massive waves ended up devouring everybody surfing in the ocean that day. And a number of homes below were wiped out. I felt I had access to infinite power and had finally tapped into the source of all power, the hidden power behind nature. Yet I had not even seen the "clear light"—that was an indication to me of how great that clear light was. It was the cosmic carrot on the end of the stick."

The trip ended, and Jeff wandered back home down the old dirt road bordering the jungle. Since then, many of those who were members of Jeff's Hawaiian Timothy Leary LSD group, who claimed to see the "clear light," have died. Jeff now realizes that the "clear light" is one of Satan's secrets. A doorway to possession.

Jeff concludes, "After my dream life of searching for

God in Hawaii fell through, and I thought I was losing my mind, I tried to leave as soon as possible. The honey sweet drink of finding bliss in nature turned bitter. I finally sold my surfboard to help get my ticket home—aided by financial help from my parents. I felt like the eunuch who went to Jerusalem to find God, but left empty-handed. I was burned out by drugs and was homesick."

Once he was back home on the mainland Jeff took another radical turn. He decided to abandon the search for God. He decided to try the straight world. "I will do what everybody says is the source of happiness." His new ambition was the American dream: a split-level home, wife, kids, a van, and even a dog—all made to order. That was the answer he now needed to fill the void inside of himself, he thought. And Jeff made it all happen. He even got a regular job for a while. "Here I was in my white picket-fenced home with a little dog, a good job, a child, and a wife." But the result was anguish as great as he had felt in Hawaii.

With all of his options burning out, Jeff was entering despair. An old friend came by and gave him a big black ball of Indian hashish laced with opium. Jeff felt the pull to turn back to drugs, and it began to fray the edges of his marriage. He knew there was a time fuse on his life. Something had to happen. While Jeff was smoking his hashish pipe one evening, he looked up at Karyn, his wife. She looked back at him and said, "Is this all that life is about? This is a bummer." Divorce looked inevitable. The American dream was crumbling and the returning drug world was no better.

Then one night another old friend, a big drug supplier, walked through his door—not with drugs but with a Bible in his hand. With fierce conviction he told Jeff how Christ had entered his life and how he had given up the deadly road of drugs. Jeff was stunned. This was not some naïve churchgoer with whom he could not identify, but one of his own kind, a heavyweight. His sincerity was undeniable. He even looked different. Jeff could feel powerful love coming from him. Finally, to placate his old friend, Jeff agreed to go with him to that evening's church service.

That night Jeff Johnson, former West Coast drug dealer and user, lawbreaker, and rebel, whose occult experiments had brought him to the brink of oblivion, walked forward to accept Jesus Christ as his Lord and Savior. He knew he was hearing the Truth. He had tried everything else and it had all been seductive falsehood, sideshow games that had been rigged. The words of Christ had the ring of eternal truth.

Jeff changed dramatically and immediately. The Bible, which Jeff could never quite understand, now started to make incredible sense that very night. From then on he pored over its pages, absorbing its great truths. Why had he not seen it all before? Because his mind was previously darkened. God had to open Jeff's eyes.

Jeff's changes were so intense, in his life and character, that within six months, his wife finally left. He was no longer the same man. In fact she even preferred his drug excesses over his newfound passion. He was worse as a zealot for Christ than as a doper, as far as she was concerned. His zeal for the Lord was boundless. Indeed, perhaps it was a little too raw-edged, too insensitive to the acceptable boundaries of others and needed to be tempered.

Within two weeks of Jeff's conversion, he started to come to Calvary Chapel Costa Mesa regularly. He came for four years and sat under my teaching, after which he felt equipped to start his own church. We had been through the Bible twice by then. Jeff was an avid learner and passionate apologist for the faith.

When Jeff's wife had first separated from him, he joined up with six other fellows and started a Christian commune in Downey, a suburb of Los Angeles. It was called the Philadelphia House, and sixty to eighty high school youth were coming there each night to hear Jeff teach. But the local neighbors were suspicious, connecting it to a Manson-type cult. The police would come almost nightly with helicopters and car raids, but all they ever found were serious disciples avidly sharing their faith.

At this time Karyn was off with another man and back into drugs and partying, though she confessed to Jeff later that she felt absolutely empty inside. He was praying for her, but he was not about to return to that lifestyle. He had found reality, finally. Meanwhile, Karyn had even found a counselor, a "professional," who agreed with her that Jeff was brainwashed, fanatical, and should be divorced. But Karyn did come back and they spent months working very hard on reconciliation, going to marriage counseling, and doing a lot of praying and communicating together.

After those four years of attending Calvary Chapel Costa Mesa, Jeff and Karyn's marriage was healthy and grounded. The Lord had guided them through their initial problems and growing pains. But these were not completely over yet. The pastorate would extract unanticipated demands.

Jeff began to feel that he had a mission in his hometown. He felt called to be a pastor. He also knew that Downey needed a church similar to Calvary Chapel. So for a year, Jeff became the part-time, unofficial youth pastor at a church in Downey. But soon Jeff became distressed over all of the politics, inefficiency, back-stabbing, and manipulation that he saw there. The church was not reaching the huge needs of Downey, which he termed "a spiritual desert." Meanwhile Jeff's weeknight Bible study was drawing more people than the pastor's, and envy resulted. The pastor closed down Jeff's study for a while until requests of the parishioners brought it back. Time and again he would be grieved no end as he saw God's work actually hampered from within that church—the very vessel that should be bringing the truth to the world. It was a tragic irony.

One evening God indicated to Jeff that he was to leave the church and begin a Calvary Chapel. He was to start from scratch.

So, in May of 1973, he began what was to become Calvary Chapel of Downey in Furman Park! It was simple and natural. His first turnout was ten people. There was not the slightest indication of the staggering size that this fellowship would one day become. Jeff felt that Downey was his area, given to him by God. But there were some things Jeff still had to learn before the real harvest came.

When the rainy season arrived, Jeff was given a feeling by the Spirit of where to drive to look for his new building—Downey Avenue and Fourth Street. And there it was: an old store. It could hold a hundred per service. Jeff says of this era in his ministry: "This is the place where God started to show me—for two-and-a-half years—what it was to be a pastor and how to have a shepherd's heart. What it was to have a commitment to people, to love them, to teach them, and to learn to trust the Lord to do his work. This was my spiritual wilderness where God really dealt with me and only then did we gradually start to grow. By the end of those two-and-a-half years, we were up to two hundred people."

Then the harvest for Downey began. Jeff and the Downey Calvary Chapel started to move to different facilities as the fellowship grew. One day, in March of 1977, his church accountant told Jeff prophetically, "You will need to find a building that will seat fifteen hundred people." At the time, this comment seemed preposterous.

But sure enough, as Jeff was driving down the freeway one day, his eye was drawn to the Downey Civic Center, a big multimillion dollar theater that held 750. He felt that he should at least go through the motions of trying to get it for Sunday mornings. When he expected the manager to laugh in his face in response to using it, he heard instead a cheerful "That will be no problem." But when Jeff walked out on the stage and saw the large auditorium his response was, "Oh, no. I can't do this Lord." God assured Jeff that it would be done through Him and that no man would get the glory, but God alone.

Soon after the accountant's prophetic remark, Jeff started services in the Downey Civic Center. Six months later, the crowds were so great that Jeff was forced to hold two services on Sunday mornings. And that equalled 1,500 people, as the prophecy had foretold.

But Jeff was facing a hidden foe that has been a classical stumblingblock to pastors for centuries. It may be the greatest bane, the most difficult obstacle that any pastor faces. It has also undone many a ministry. I am referring to the needs of one's own family that conflict with what seem the infinite needs of one's church. Indeed Jeff's ministry was becoming a desert experience to those whom he loved the most, his family.

Jeff has told audiences what was at stake. He says:

"During all this growth and busy time with the church, I had gotten into an affair. Not with a woman, but with the church. My family was suffering, especially my wife. She was going through some real changes. And my being gone so much did not help matters. She started to withdraw after a hard experience in a women's group. She was crying a lot and I thought that she just needed more Bible and fellowship (the convenient 'easy answer'), but in reality she was on the verge of a nervous breakdown. We found out years later that Karyn had a fear of crowds. I was at my wit's end.

"Finally, my wife and I went to an old friend for marriage counseling. That is when God hit me with Acts 1:8, that I was not taking care of 'Jerusalem' first. My home was my ministry, my church was my calling. I preached it, told young couples about it, but I was failing to do this myself. I had to repent and change my actions to love my wife as Christ loved the Church. Ever since then, our marriage has been growing and getting stronger. And one more thing, my wife beat the phobia with God's help."

Jeff also faced problems with the Civic Center. Special events would override the church's use of the auditorium. It seemed to put Jeff into an impossible situation. How do you get any bigger than the local civic center? What around was any bigger?

Once Jeff faced his family problems, with God's help, God proved once again that He is able to solve impossible situations. Jeff was now ready for the next thing God had in store for his ministry.

If you have ever seen the largest of the Target stores, they are almost the size of an indoor mall. In California we had a chain, where the stores were perhaps even bigger than Target, called "White Front." The one in Downey, which was no longer being used, was stupendous. It had twelve acres just for parking cars.

In May 1978, only five years after Jeff had started his small fellowship in Furman Park, Calvary Chapel of Downey moved into the colossal facility—150,000 square feet under a single roof. That equals three football fields!

On February 8, 1980, a year-and-a-half after they moved into the massive new facility, the Los Angeles *Times* did a feature article on this church, headlined "Downey's Largest," in its section on Southeast News. They mentioned the 1,500-seat sanctuary that was being built, and the fact that a total of 5,000 were showing up Sunday mornings during the three overflow services. Some of the building space was being set aside for a school.

The *Times* article began with the words, "The growth of Calvary Chapel, located in an old White Front store at Woodruff and Imperial highways in Downey, can only be considered phenomenal." A picture of Jeff in front of the facility was featured. In the month before the article was written, the attendance of the church, according to the staff writer, had increased by five hundred people. In that single month, the church gained twice the number of members that Jeff had in his first two years of ministry.

Today the church is still growing. Plans have just been approved to build a 4,000-seat sanctuary. But Jeff disavows that it is from any charisma on his part—he is an onlooker. It is God who is allowing this to happen. Jeff feels that he is called to be faithful and not look to himself but to God and try to meet people's needs.

When Jeff speaks it is from a grounding in both worldly experience and heavenly wisdom. He is warm and he is transparently honest. The church members know that one who talks about his own battles with lust or unbelief is anything but a spiritual phony.

Jeff's eyes are on the contemporary battles of our society. For instance he erred in junior high school and he knows exactly what young people are going through when they become parents outside of marriage. Since both Jeff and Karyn have been an unwed father and mother themselves, they have a burden for unwed mothers. So they started the House of Ruth for them. He addresses this contemporary problem on the air. He counsels people in these dilemmas who face tough choices: should a pregnant high school girl, who has become a Christian, try to marry the teenaged father, bring up her baby alone, or give it to a responsible couple for adoption? And if she is not a Christian, how do you get her to see that abortion is murder and something that she will have to live with the rest of her life? These are some of the issues that Jeff's ministry has had to address.

And what about drugs? He talks about this problem sometimes during Sunday services, and on the radio, and has a ministry for people with drug problems where they can dry out. The ministry also counsels people with a variety of critical problems: those who are in the middle of domestic disputes, those on the brink of suicide, or those who have OD'd on drugs.

There are other ministries—a theater company, concerts, movies, a nationwide daily radio ministry called "Sound Doctrine," various missions outreaches and support, meal services, shelter, a prison ministry, family counseling, and evangelistic crusades, to name only a few. Jeff has been called to speak all over the world, he has given pastors' conferences in Egypt and other parts of Africa, where he has also spoken at Gospel crusades.

Jeff acts on his strong conviction that the Church is the world's primary agent holding out the bright light of God's revelation, truth, and grace while living out the Gospel of Jesus Christ in faith and action. Its highest allegiance must be a supernatural one first of all, then the love of God can shine through a variety of actions.

To get it all in perspective, picture once again that nude youth running through the jungles of Oahu on LSD and rat poison in the hands of occult powers; picture a former drug pusher who showed such signs of utter incorrigibility that everyone gave up on him from the third grade onward. He had to forge the records just to graduate from high school. And organized crime was at his door.

Now picture him with the colossal ministry outreach of an overflowing church in Downey.

Can this magnitude of change in a person's character and life be anything short of an act of God?

Could Karl Marx or Sigmund Freud change such a life from the inside out? Hardly. For, you see, though Marx could give someone a "cause," and though Freud might make that cause an "understanding" of one's self, neither could fill the inner void of a soul with love. Love is the great miracle, the missing ingredient in all these "causes." Such love is a supernatural gift of divine grace from a sovereign God.

Ask Jeff Johnson where this love came from, ask the blind man who now sees. And from Jeff's own mouth you hear the words, "Jesus Christ, the Savior of the world, entered me one day, forgave my untold sins, and then changed me forever." Only God's Messiah can do that, and that is part of the mystery of why He came.

9

Skip Heitzig: Calvary Chapel Enters the Southwest

In 1981 there was no Calvary Chapel in the state of New Mexico. Today the massive Calvary Chapel of Albuquerque has become the largest church in the state. It started out as a Bible study, then became a church, and started moving from facility to facility as it grew. Finally the fellowship bought "The Sports Center," a huge complex with an indoor soccer field, racquetball courts, and offices. They installed 1,700 seats on the soccer field after pulling up the astro turf and replacing it with carpet. It was hoped that this new facility was now big enough to allow them to hold only one Sunday morning service. But from the moment the renovated complex opened, the crowds spilled over into two Sunday morning services. Attendance at Calvary Chapel of Albuquerque jumped to 4,000 adults on the first day in this new facility!

The instrument God used in this is Skip Heitzig, a handsome six-foot-four fellow. All Skip knew, from the time he became a Christian in the early '70s, and faithfully attended and worked with Calvary Chapel, was that he was supposed to leave California one day and plant a church. Later on he knew it was to be somewhere in the Southwest. In 1981 Skip and his wife moved to Albuquerque and Skip started a Bible study. There was a period of intense trial, but from then on it grew.

If you look at Skip today, he looks as straight as they come. You would never guess his past. That alone testifies to what the Holy Spirit can do in a believer's life. Skip grew up in the high desert country of Southern California, reaching his mid-teens when the '60s turned into the '70s. He was going along a peculiar and dangerous road when the Lord stood at an intersection to hail him down.

PLAYING WITH PSYCHIC POWERS

In 1971 Skip and Gino, a close friend, were both sixteen and in high school. They had broken away from the rest of their high school tour group, and were camping out in a hotel room in Mazatlan, a subtropical region along Mexico's Pacific coast. From there they hoped to contact the spirit world.

Gino had a reputation for reading people's fortunes with tarot cards. But their goal was to get the spirits to take them over and write messages through them by "automatic writing." They both sat in their hotel room for a couple of nights waiting to make contact.

Skip was in a trance. His hand held a pen poised over a piece of paper. He was sending out messages, asking the spirits to take control of his arm and write messages about his past lives. Was he a former Atlantean high priest or Indian mystic?

Mazatlan's damp night ocean air started howling

through the windows. The curtains flapped. An electric presence seemed to fill the air. Skip's arm started moving out of his control. The pen scribbled meaninglessly for a while. Then words started to form: "You were in the Franco-Prussian war where you were killed." Skip and Gino were alarmed, then frightened. What had they summoned? Then the spirit gave him a message: "Skip, you are going to die on your way home from Mazatlan." Now they were scared to death. After a few hours, well past midnight, they lay in their beds trying to go to sleep, occasionally discussing what it meant. Would they really be killed on the train journey back to California?

In the early hours of the morning a light caught Skip's attention. A shining thing was bouncing up and down the wall. It seemed to be part of the message. He cried out to Gino and they discovered that moonlight was reflecting off a dagger that laid by Skip's bedside. They did not know how the dagger got there. Skip suddenly understood: "We're going to get knifed to death on the train!" For a while, they refused to go back home. Then, when they finally agreed to return with the group, nothing happened.

With the idea of reincarnation Skip felt a new freedom. If he had endless lifetimes before him to experience things, he could throw each one away like a cigarette. There would always be another life. So why not try new thrills? He and his rock band started to burn entire lids of Acapulco gold marijuana in a sealed-off practice room. One night he and a friend took off on a new adventure. Hours later they were in a police station, busted for grand larceny. His father grounded him for a month, but he smiled inwardly. Skip had rarely been happier than when he was committing the crime. He figured that God wanted him happy, and that crime made him happy, so God approved it. He also kept pursuing his quest for psychic powers. In trances he would find items that he had lost for years. He would be "guided" to where they were. A whole new realm was opening before him.

Then Skip started studying about astral projection. He learned to lie in a trance, his body paralyzed, a loud buzzing sound in his ear. Suddenly he would discorporate and seem to leave his body behind. At one point Skip and Gino decided to meet as spirits in the lobby of the Mazatlan Hotel. They compared notes, after sensing each other there: They had seen similar faces in the bar.

Skip's next experiment was geared to impress a girl who was "Miss Victorville" and a model, now a fellow student in his high school photography class. "I can project into your bedroom," he challenged. She laughed in his face. So he vowed to show her.

Skip lay back in his bedroom, went into a trance, and seemed to discorporate as he willed himself into her bedroom. He saw her reading in bed, examined her room, the red curtains, and then tried to leave a mental message that he was there.

Back in class he told her the entire layout of her room, the moment he had appeared, and that he had seen her reading. She looked horrified. Then he said he had been hovering near the foot of her bed. She reported that at that exact time, she looked on the floor and saw a flat piece of paper suddenly crumple up into a ball on the floor. "That was me," Skip replied with a knowing smile. "I knew something made you aware that I was there in spirit." She covered her mouth then said, "You're weird. Get out of here."

The base drummer in the band tried astral projecting on

LSD and almost got killed by running into oncoming traffic. He thought he was a spirit while still in his body. Some years later, he was busted for selling half-a-million dollars worth of synthetic heroin.

Meanwhile Skip's hatred for his father, an aloof and demanding perfectionist who had shown him little affection from as far back as he could remember, was becoming pathological. Skip was beginning to plot his father's death. He also enjoyed giving his mother sadistic little messages like, "Mom, I hate Dad and I'm going to kill him."

His father fully expected Skip to be class valedictorian, like his two oldest brothers. Like them, Skip was ordered to follow a tight academic regimen while shooting nine holes of golf daily and learning public speech, all in a well-planned pursuit of a successful career. But no effort of Skip's was ever enough to earn his father's approval, so he stopped trying. Instead Skip viewed this sterile plan with scorn, choosing instead to shock his parents. Nor was Skip the only son to rebel against this cold disciplinarian. He had a brother Bob, two years older, who was six-foot-eight and a member of the Hell's Angels. Apparently he was brilliant, but thought of his father with contempt. One time the father slapped Bob. In turn Bob knocked him through a door and sent him flying down the hallway. Bob, like Skip, left home while still in his teens. When he was twenty-four, he was killed in a motorcycle crash.

THE ETERNAL DIVIDE

By the time Skip was eighteen and on the verge of attending San Jose State in 1973, which he really didn't want to do, his life was going nowhere and he knew it. Skip had tried everything—all the thrills of Southern California, from drugs to surfing to rock-and-roll—and it left him bored and frustrated. None of these things gave him what they promised, happiness. Skip could find no clear hold on what he should do. And the psychic channels were like a minefield. For every item of value he came up with, he had to sort through heaps of garbage that came along with it.

Skip was spending the summer in the house of one of his two older "successful" brothers who lived in San Jose, Northern California. It was a quick drive from San Francisco and its East Bay counterparts of Berkeley and Oakland. Unlike the high desert, the summers here were gloriously cool, the air full of evergreen smells. Within an hour Skip could ride his motorcycle to the Stanford campus, or be on the other side of the bay where the motley crew along Telegraph Avenue flowed onto the radical campus of UC Berkeley.

One day Skip sat alone watching TV. The one thing Skip did learn to prize from his father was the art of good communication. He was mesmerized by the face of a man on TV addressing a packed stadium. His blue eyes pierced through the screen. His voice echoed soul-searching questions, then paused with dignity. The words electrified Skip with things he had never heard or considered before.

It was Billy Graham and Skip felt as if the voice were cutting into him, peeling away his detached critical edge. The meaning of the words now began to convict him. For the first time in his life, Skip Heitzig was hearing the Gospel of Jesus Christ through the mouth of probably the greatest evangelist of our era. Skip sensed he had a choice that he did not really want to face. He considered turning the TV off before the clincher came, some question about commitment. But he waited and suddenly realized that he was glad to be sitting home alone and not out there in the open stadium where hundreds were coming forward. He knew that if he were there, he would probably be walking up the aisle himself. But he was safe, no one could see him.

Then the piercing eyes looked into the camera at the TV audience. "Wherever you are, whether you are in a bar, or a hotel room"—Skip's stomach knotted—"you too can turn your life over to Jesus Christ, right there where you are. You can kneel down and pray the sinner's prayer." Graham echoed the words of the sinner's prayer. And Skip, within the inner chambers of his soul, did the same. He was now doing what he said he would not do. Skip thought to himself: *Lord, You're getting a rotten deal. I'm giving You all this crudeness and meaninglessness in me. And You're giving me eternal life in return and blessing me. I would have to be an idiot to turn it down.* He was kneeling and praying. In a mere moment, a million-pound weight was removed from him.

Within a matter of days Skip Heitzig was on his motorcycle making the nine-hour ride from the Bay Area back to Southern California. He quit the new job he had just gotten and withdrew from college. He felt joy for the first time in his life, real joy, as he sang the whole way home.

Once in the high desert of Victorville he met one of his old friends who was at the Macedonia House, one of the Calvary Chapel communes that my brother Paul Smith directed with Steve Mays. Skip's friend was now a Christian. He immediately asked Skip, "Have you been born again?" Suddenly there was a word that described what had happened to him. And there was even a Scripture for it, John 3. His soul had been washed and made new. Skip had changed and been given a new nature.

From then on Skip worked with Macedonia House and got grounded in the faith. He found out that a number of his old friends had been converted and had been praying for him. On Sundays Skip would come down from the high desert to Calvary Chapel Costa Mesa to hear me teach. My brother soon got Skip into a situation where he was forced to teach a Bible study. And that was when Skip discovered he had a gift.

Skip kept plugging into various Calvary Chapels after he moved from the Macedonia House to San Bernardino where he worked on a two-year degree in radiology. I had told him that for ministers starting a church, it was not a bad idea to have an occupation that you can take with you anywhere in order to underwrite your ministry. Skip got his degree in 1975. Then he moved near Calvary Chapel Costa Mesa and taught Bible studies while he continued fellowshiping with us and waiting for God to direct his path in the church-planting ministry.

During these years of growth, Skip made peace with his father. It happened after his brother was killed in the motorcycle accident mentioned earlier. Skip saw his father at the funeral and knew that the Lord would have him show his father the love of Christ. He grabbed his father and said a prayer out loud: "Lord, thank You for my dad. I love him. He's been a gift to me. He's been a great dad." It stunned Skip's father as the two stood there teary-eyed. If anything could signal a change in Skip's life to his father, it was this new love and meekness. Since that time the two have grown closer. And now these two fellows who never hugged, hug every time they see each other.

Skip relates that only two weeks before his brother's death, he felt God's clear direction late one night after a Bible study. He was to go by his brother's house nearby and witness to him. His brother had always violently rejected Skip's Christianity. Skip told this bitter Hell's Angel, "You just don't know when you are going to die. Life could end anytime." And it did. Sadly his brother had only laughed.

GOD PROVIDES A MATE AND A MINISTRY

By 1978 Skip had been a Christian for seven years. He was zealous and eager, teaching and sharing anytime he could, while keeping his eye on the horizon to see where he might plant a church. He met Lenya that year at one of the church functions. When she was in college, her dad, Dr. Farley, an atheistic medical doctor, had written a book on positive thinking entitled, *How To Make Your Dreams Come True*. He had decided that Jesus might be a good example. But when he read the Bible, something happened: He became converted. Lenya soon followed her father's footsteps. Like him, she began involving herself in Calvary Chapel's ministries to learn and be built up as a disciple after having dropped out of college. Suddenly she was stopped in her tracks by this tall, handsome fellow. Lenya, a bright, good-looking girl, immediately attracted Skip's attention as well. And they dated for six months.

Then Skip backed out. He was afraid of commitment. He had seen precious little love in his own family. And he was afraid of the risks of emotional vulnerability. Besides, he told himself, he was a more mature Christian, and now a responsible leader, while Lenya was a recent convert. They just weren't on the same wavelength.

Soon after his brother died, Skip left Lenya in Orange County and headed to Israel to work on a kibbutz. In the meantime, Lenya joined Youth With A Mission and spent two years in Hawaii. She grew in her faith, but her longing to marry Skip and be a pastor's wife grew as well. To her, this was a high calling indeed. Such desires were against the tide of feminism as well as her career-oriented peers, who felt she should be "out there doing something." But Lenya knew where her heart was. Skip was her dream husband, friend, and companion.

Her father knew all about his daughter's yearning. Now if it wasn't going to happen, Dr. Farley wanted to end the uncertainty for Lenya's sake, so that she would know and be able to get on with her life. He did something rare for modern fathers these days.

Skip had decided that the Lord wanted him to start his church in New Mexico. Just when he was on the verge of moving in 1981, Dr. Farley called him. "Skip, I love my daughter enough to make this call and tell you what she would never tell you. Skip, she is in love with you. If you love her, too, I want you to tell her. You owe it to her to tell her how you feel. If you do not love her, then tell her you do not want anything to do with her. But let her know either way, so she can get on with her life." Skip was stunned. Like the old days, the father was looking after his daughter and almost arranging a marriage. Skip could only reply, "I didn't know she loved me."

Skip moved tentatively. He sent her a fishy, rambling letter with a picture of himself holding a surfboard. She wrote back a letter so vulnerable and self-revealing that a friend had to mail it for her. In it she came right out with her desire to marry Skip, to be a pastor's wife, and to move to a new area. Skip read it trembling. He felt his own heart being expressed by her words. He sent her a bouquet of flowers. His follow-up letter a week later said, "I love you."

Lenya returned in the spring of 1981 from Hawaii and Skip was there to meet her, holding a rose for her. They drove straight to the beach to pray. Then they talked nonstop for three days. Within two months, on June 13, 1981, they were married, and two weeks after that, they moved to Albuquerque.

All of these changes at once—a new marriage, new job for Skip in radiology, new ministry (a Bible study in their apartment), new town—put a lot of pressure on the couple. On top of everything else Skip was depressed by the weather. He was used to Southern California winters in the mid-seventies, full of sunny days and blue skies. Somehow, he had not considered the weather before making the move. In fact they were both under a lot of stress, causing them to both cry almost every day for a while.

Skip had promised God a year in New Mexico, but he decided that six months was enough. When they took a Christmas vacation in California Skip said, "Lenya, I belong back here." But Lenya was apprehensive about leaving. Then God spoke to Skip's heart, *You owe me six months*, and Skip knew it was true.

Reluctantly he returned to New Mexico. Skip now says that those next six months were the most incredible six months of his life.

Right before Valentine's Day of 1982, they started Sunday services in a movie theater. This was just after

Raul Ries had come to town and held a crusade. Skip was sure the spacious movie theater would be empty, but 150 showed up. By June all 300 of the seats were filled on Sunday mornings. They moved to a renovated storefront with 400 seats, and within a few months, by September, they had to remodel it to seat 550. By 1983 they had to switch to two services.

Next they moved to a shopping center with a facility that would seat 900. That was in 1984. They stayed there two years, again doubling to two services. When the landlord made conditions intolerable, because of his violently anti-Christian stance, the way opened for them to buy the Sports Center. Every obstacle was swept aside, and with each change of course Skip saw his fellowship grow into a bountiful harvest.

Today Skip and Lenya have deeply fulfilled lives with a happy family and a healthy church. Skip is on the radio daily in New Mexico and other regions. Gino, Skip's high school friend, is now a Christian and a staff member of the church. From out of Calvary Chapel of Albuquerque have sprung a number of churches, including Calvary Chapels in Tucson and Denver, and four other churches in New Mexico. Skip and Lenya's burden for the mission field is fulfilled as well. Skip has gone to India to give pastors' conferences. And they now plan to build a mission school in the mountains above Albuquerque.

Those demonic spirits that moved Skip's arm in the Mazatlan hotel room could only offer him death threats. But the sovereign God who moved Skip's entire life has brought him a richness and depth of life, a hope and a joy, a quality of being, and a harvest of souls, that have surpassed Skip's wildest imaginings.

God also brought him a beautiful wife who loves her

Lord and her husband. She has brought beauty to Skip's life and enriched it. She has helped make all the difference in the world to his ministry.

Skip listened to God at each turn, and let Him built his life into something that no personal strategy could have ever accomplished. In this tapestry of lives, we see a former psychic becoming a great vessel of the Lord. He who was once influenced by demonic spirits is now governed and indwelt by the Holy Spirit. These two states, as Skip will tell you, are a universe apart, as the fruit of Skip's life, before and after, clearly shows.

As Paul the apostle was relating his conversion experience to King Agrippa, he said that Jesus sent him to the Gentiles to turn them from darkness to light, from the power of Satan to God. This describes what happened to Skip. He testifies to others that there is no life so dark that the light of Jesus cannot shine in and cleanse and make new.

10

"Bil" Gallatin & Joe Focht: Calvary Chapel Pushes East

PART 1: BIL GALLATIN IN UPSTATE NEW YORK

Calvary Chapel fellowships, large fellowships at that, are by no means just a West Coast phenomenon anymore. The harvest that we have seen in the Western United States is now beginning to appear in the Midwest, the Southwest, and now the East Coast.

It has been particularly heartening to see East Coasters laying aside apprehension about a "non-traditional" church like Calvary Chapel and opening their doors and hearts to our fellowships. I think the stories of "Bil" Gallatin and Joe Focht illustrate beautifully the willingness to let go of formality and tradition in favor of letting the fresh breeze of the Spirit blow in. Bil and Joe moved east with their mustard seed faith, prayed for God's grace, persevered, then watched it happen; and God brought in the harvest. As always, they started with a Bible study and then watched it grow into a church.

Just recently I flew back from an East Coast pastors' conference in Upstate New York where perhaps a hundred of our East Coast ministers attended. We were only a few miles from Bil Gallatin's Maranatha Fellowship, where I spoke in the evenings. It was a thrilling experience to see what is happening in these fellowships. We even ordained a fellow who is on the philosophy faculty at West Point who has started a Calvary Chapel fellowship right there. Pastors came in from Pennsylvania, New Jersey, Illinois, North Carolina, Georgia, South Carolina, Ohio, Tennessee, Virginia, and New York City, where, as was mentioned earlier, we have a fellowship in Manhattan meeting in a dance studio with up to five hundred members. Greg Laurie, pastor of the Harvest Fellowship at Riverside, flew to New York a few years ago to help start the Manhattan fellowship.

If we examine the East Coast growth of Calvary Chapel, I would have to point to Bil Gallatin's Maranatha Fellowship near the city of Rochester, New York, as the key foundational fellowship. It has been a kind of home base for many of the other Calvary Chapels, while Bil has been an inspiration and a voice of encouragement to many starting fellowships.

Maranatha Fellowship exploded in a ten-year period. It meets in a roller skating rink that will seat well over a thousand, and has three morning services on Sundays.

Ten years ago Bil Gallatin was on staff at Calvary Chapel Costa Mesa as a carpenter. Before that he was a construction worker, college dropout, and one time hippie.

When Bil was converted in early 1970, this 220-pound man with a thick beard and long hair showed up in denim overalls. He had recently sold his .357 magnum revolver. Bil was no one you wanted to mess around with.

Bil ended his brief attendance at Bowling Green State University, Ohio, in the late '50s, when he beat somebody senseless on campus. With a warrant out on him, he fled and joined the Marines. When Bil got out in 1960, he married Rosemary, but continued drinking and getting into fights. He worked various jobs in Ohio while his marriage went down the skids. In 1968 Bil and Rosemary looked to California for sunshine and hope and new identities. It was there that Bil discovered psychedelics and the occult. After that he was ready to meet Jesus Christ. When Bil walked into my office in early 1970, the countercultural phenomenon had reached its peak.

A month or so before I first saw this wild-eyed man, Bil Gallatin had been on one of his last psychedelic trips. Bil had been sitting in a coastal cemetery overlooking the Pacific Ocean near Corona Del Mar, when he beheld a vision that he described to me as the end of the world. The coastline was consumed in nuclear fire, and he saw everything being destroyed. A terrible smog sat over Santa Catalina Island. Atomic bombs went off in series from there down to Los Angeles. America sank like the Titanic. The vision convinced Bil that modern man did not have the answers to existence, that as a steward of the world, he was blundering and destroying all that he touched.

A few weeks after this experience Bil accepted Christ. But he wanted a Christian to talk to, so he ended up driving into our parking lot and walking right up to me. Bil had a long way to go before he was fully healed, but he had taken a strong step of faith. He was sure that Christ was the Son of God. But we need to back up and see where his trouble began.

A CASE OF POSSESSION

Ironically, as we will see with Mike MacIntosh, Bil had also been locked up in a psychiatric holding tank for a few weeks. When Bil went there with his wife he was sure they were going to keep her. But they kept him instead, strapping him down and wheeling him through huge metal doors. This was grim humor indeed. Rosemary was later told he was a hopeless case and that she had better get used to the fact that he would probably not be coming out. His long months of bizarre behavior—evident telepathy, imaginary visitors for dinner, and long binges on mescaline and LSD—had taken their toll.

But the real problem was not mental; it was spiritual, demonic. There were times that the violence Rosemary felt lurking beneath Bil's powerful presence seemed almost volcanic. He had a long history of fights, necessitating that she go down and get him out of jail time and again. In truth she had sensed something alien inside of Bil, but she had no idea what it was. Neither of them knew anything about the reality of demonic possession, though Bil had been afraid that something terrible was going on inside of him.

He remembered when it began. He was on a week-long drug binge in Baja, Mexico, in early 1968. He and a small group of friends on the beach explored the outer limits of freedom. It was then that he saw an image of Satan in the beach bonfire one night. It was hideously beautiful and captivating. Its message to Bil was, "Don't be afraid. There is nothing in the world to be afraid of."

Some months after that—Bil had been on psychedelics for three days—he walked into his house, stood in the doorway of the kitchen, and stared Rosemary in the eyes.

She was terrified. An overpowering swooning force thrust down his spine, knocking Bil on his back. Something entered him. He felt a new power inside of him. Suddenly he could read Rosemary's mind. He had access to any of her thoughts and she could no longer keep secrets. As he got off the kitchen floor and stood up again in the doorway, his eyes and appearance seemed to change dramatically. From that time on, for two years, Rosemary lived in fear.

Bil refers to his exorcism as a sovereign act of God. It took place in the kitchen of a nearby house they had moved to. No one else was there. Bil had been reading the Bible, and experiencing considerable adversity while doing this. At two in the afternoon—this was two years after the original possession and a short time after he realized that Jesus was the Son of God—Bil was suddenly knocked flat on his back.

As he lay on the kitchen floor, Bil convulsed and twisted helplessly. The thought pressed in on his mind: *There is no hope for me. This is it. I'm finished*. Then he suddenly called upon the name of Jesus. Bil mouthed the words, "Jesus, help me!"

Bil's body suddenly became motionless as something seemed to expel out of him. He lay absolutely still. Then a peace entered him that was incredible. For the first time in his life, Bil felt as though a heavy weight had been taken off of him. Then he noticed that his sweat-drenched garments had an absolutely hideous stench to them. Bil spent hours in the shower. It was at the exorcism, Bil claims, that God saved him. When Rosemary came home she found a different man. But that frightened her even more. Not long after that, she plotted to take him to the holding tank for psychiatric observation. But God had a plan even in this.

Bil's doctor while he spent two weeks in the holding tank was Dr. Clarence Jones. He had just accepted Christ and started coming to Calvary Chapel. One thing that impressed the doctor was that even under massive doses of Stellazine, they could not in any way subdue Bil's excited proclamations about Christ. Indeed they became frightened of this powerful figure who kept announcing to them, "Jesus is coming!" This apparently had an effect on Dr. Jones. He even came to debate me in order to prove that the agnostic viewpoint was the only viable option for "realists."

Dr. Jones is now a Messianic Jew. Soon after he had Bil released, he saw Bil at one of the Calvary Chapel services. Dr. Jones suddenly turned around to see a smiling and sane Bil Gallatin sitting right behind him. Then he announced to Bil, "Don't worry about the medical fees, I've got them covered."

RECOVERY, GROWTH, AND GUIDANCE

For seven years Bil Gallatin attended Calvary Chapel Costa Mesa, learning diligently. He couldn't seem to get enough. He exulted over the change of his life's destiny. Scars in him slowly healed as Bil prayed fervently, worshiped, fellowshiped, joined the staff for a year as a carpenter, and led the evening Afterglow services. But by the summer of 1977, God had just about gotten Bil where He wanted him. Bil was being prepared for the task of pioneering Calvary Chapel back East.

For those who wonder how God "speaks" to individuals, Bil's experience of God directing him provides a clear example. We hear about counterfeits of this all the time, and cults are rife with false guidance. But that does not disprove the genuine leading of God. I am not speaking about "new revelation" or doctrines. For anything in the area of revelatory truth "beyond" or added to Scripture is heresy: The canon of completed Scripture has indeed been given once and for all to all the saints. I am talking about God guiding our lives when He so chooses. To say that God cannot lead us these days is to put Him in a box. The Bible is loaded with very clear examples of God leading individuals, groups, and nations in particular situations. But the final test of God's genuine leading, as God pointed out to Moses in Deuteronomy, is that the results are borne out in history. It happens! In Bil's case, what looked impossible from a human perspective indeed took place.

First of all there came the inward nudges. Bil began to feel pulled toward the ministry. His impact at Afterglow services was significant. In his heart there grew a strong desire to teach the Word of God. At the same time Bil was feeling limited at Calvary Chapel in the daily routines of his carpentry work. Meanwhile there were other capacities in him on hold. Bil was pulling desperately at the bit.

Then the first arrow from God's quiver seemed to strike home. Bil was having a prayer meeting with two classmates from Calvary's first Shepherd School, Mike MacIntosh and Keith Ritter. Keith suddenly announced, "I have a vision from the Lord and it is about Bil." Keith described a pastoral scene out of picture-book New England. "I see a tall silo almost filled to the top with grain. It is surrounded by farm animals. I get the impression of 'farm.' There is also a carriage or covered wagon in the setting." Mike was given the interpretation: The silo represented Bil as the feeder of the animals, which stood for the flock of believers that God had waiting for him. Bil was almost full of "grain" and ready to feed. The location was in some farm territory outside of California, maybe out East.

One day, a month or so after this, Bil was working on our new parking lot. As clear and as certain as anything Bil had ever heard came a voice: "I want you to go to the Finger Lakes." Immediately Bil started to weep, because he knew it was from God. Bil had been to Upstate New York as a young man, when his dad had lived in Rochester. The Finger Lakes were in Upstate New York.

Rosemary was horrified. She became a Christian two years after Bil, but she didn't really want to leave California, and if she did, she wanted to make sure it was really God leading. "I'll have to see it in the Bible." The next evening at Calvary Chapel's Thursday night service, a girl sitting in front of them, whom Rosemary knew, suddenly turned around to Bil and Rosemary. She said to Rosemary, "This may seem strange, but I feel that the Lord is giving me a passage to tell you. It is Deuteronomy chapter eight."

It was Bil's fortieth birthday. Amazingly, the passage was addressed to Moses when he had turned forty. In it God said to Moses that He had tested him those forty years, and was sending him into a land of hills, lakes, springs, wheat, and barley. That is the passage that convinced them. Bil was now certain that for him to resist God's clear indications to move to New York would be to invite a kind of spiritual death. The case was sealed the next morning when they woke up in their Newport Beach house to see the owner hammering a *For Sale* sign in front of the house.

Three weeks later on July 7, 1977 (Bil notes the date as 7/7/77—seven representing God's perfect will, among other things), Bil and Rosemary Gallatin arrived in Upstate New York in a beat-up old Chevy containing two kids, all their worldly goods, and a German shepherd. Bill had eight-five cents in his pocket. They landed in *Farm*ington and moved into a townhouse with a clear view of a solitary silo near them.

This marked the beginning of a new Calvary Chapel. And it was tough going. Some locals said that Bil was a false prophet. Other divisive things were said. These blows knocked the wind out of him time and again. Bil would call me occasionally and ask to come back. I told him to keep plowing. God then told Bil that if he could persevere for three years, the harvest would come. God gave Bil a passage in Zechariah about taking His people through the fire. And for three years they just barely scraped by. Bil couldn't even fall back on his construction skills since he was suffering from torn ligaments. When friends left food on Bil and Rosemary's porch, it was like the ravens feeding the prophets.

But three years passed. Bil's burgeoning Bible study moved into an empty train depot. It would seat 150. Bil was unnerved by the size of it. But a year later, in 1981, they were having two Sunday services. A year after that they expanded the rail depot so it could hold 250 a service. They immediately had to go to three services since more than 750 people were coming on Sunday mornings. Traffic was becoming a problem for local residents. When they went to five Sunday services the heat was on for them to move.

Then Bil found the place, a town with an Indian name that means "chosen spot," Canandaigua. On Route 332, on the Farmington border, Bil had often noticed a brand-new skating rink that was not being used—it did not have enough people coming to it to make it financially viable, so it had been closed. In no time he purchased the 26,000-square-foot facility with no down payment!

Now here is the miracle of the harvest: In the first three weeks that they opened the refurbished skating rink—with over a thousand seats—they were forced to go to three services to make room for everyone. That was in 1984. Today Maranatha Fellowship continues to grow. In addition Bil has been able to start four spin-off churches in nearby Rochester and neighboring areas.

A stone's throw from the church stands a tall silo in the town of Farmington. History has borne out the vision that God provided at that prayer meeting. God's many proddings to get Bil Gallatin where he was called to minister have brought astounding results. Calvary Chapel has seen great harvest in Upstate New York, where it already has become one of the largest churches in the region. And Bil is a deeply contented man. He has come a staggering distance from that kitchen floor, where he was set free by the power of God. Even then few could have imagined this same fellow starting a church in Upstate New York. And not even a dreamer would venture to notion that such a man would one day be the humble, strong, and balanced pastor that God would use to build a church of 3,000 from scratch.

PART 2: JOE FOCHT IN PHILADELPHIA

In God's economy of purpose, it is ironic that the man he used to take Calvary Chapel to Philadelphia has more than a passing resemblance to the fictional character Rocky, whose town of "Philly" is famous for boxers. Joe Focht, a native of Philadelphia, was going for the Golden Gloves championship in the late '60s. This athletic fellow, six-foot-two with the good looks of a movie star, seemed to have it in sight to win the Gloves, when suddenly, during a fight, a spinal disk ruptured. Joe was trying to hit hard from an odd angle. He made an awkward twist and felt the snap; he went down from the pain. Overnight he got sciatica so badly that he dragged his leg and had to wear a body brace for a while. That ended Joe's boxing hopes.

Another disappointment, right before Joe had thrown himself into boxing, had been college. In 1968 Joe went to Colorado State at Fort Collins for one meaningless semester, then dropped out. It seemed hollow. Issues of ultimate meaning overshadowed the significance of his classes. Joe had gone to please his dad, but that had shallow rewards as well. Joe, typical of his generation, was alienated from both his parents.

Later, after the accident, he moved back home and felt

like an alien. Plus, because of his injury, he could no longer go around with his old group of jocks.

Joe started to look for physical healing for his back. He tried hatha yoga and his back seemed to get better. That led to other forms of yoga as he threw himself into yoga classes under his new Indian guru, Amrith Desai. Joe had a new circle of friends. Soon he was trying LSD with some of them. Then LSD and meditation. Then he added vegetarianism to his regimen and joined a rock-and-roll band. Within a year or two, his mother was virtually crying in despair. Joe was pale, had long hair, and when he sat down to talk with his dad, his dad would leave a half-hour later not understanding a word that his son had said. What had been a communication gap between Joe and his parents now took on cosmic dimensions.

In 1971, when Guru Maharaji was popular, Joe went to a New York City auditorium to hear him speak. Then Joe spent two days in a devotee's house waiting in line to be initiated by the boy guru. The experience did not impress Joe, but he incorporated Maharaji's technique of meditating under a blanket.

One day in the spring of 1972 when Joe was in meditation, he found himself running along an open field. He sensed a heavy pressure coming down on his back. Fear hit Joe as he sensed he was being pursued by some large creature with wings. When the wing flapping came close enough to hear, Joe had the distinct impression that the creature was very evil. Suddenly he fell down in the field. He called on the name of Maharaji for help and nothing happened. Something in Joe knew that he should call on the name of Jesus. He did and immediately the creature disappeared. Joe filed this away in his mind.

THE PRESENCE OF CHRIST

In the fall of 1972 Joe's rock band rented a summer estate called Innisfree Estate, at Skinner's Falls, Pennsylvania. By now Joe's mystical pursuit was obsessive. He and his best friend, Harrison, moved to the estate a month early before the rest of the band arrived. They brought hundreds of pounds of grain to eat along with wild roots and herbs that they cooked. They bathed in the cold river and spent half the night meditating. The estate had a decadent feel of opulence.

At three A.M. one morning Joe and Harrison got into an argument. Joe had been reading the Bible from time to time, and Harrison wanted to leave it behind saying, "The Bible is against everything we've been doing." But Harrison agreed to look at it one time. They threw the Bible open and their eyes fell on 1 Corinthians 11. They had been doing their meditation under blankets again. The passage read, in effect, 'Never pray with a veil over your head.' They were suddenly struck by this.

Joe describes that moment: "The presence of the Lord stepped right into the room. It was tangible. There was the overwhelming sensation of a Person—not just a power or a force. I knew it was God in Christ. Harrison felt it too. The Presence was so holy that I just hung my head. I couldn't lift it. We both started weeping. All of our previous ideas about finding nirvana were flushed out of our minds. Jesus was alive, and truly God in and of Himself. He washed all the junk away. We wept and wept as we felt His awesomely holy Presence.

"That was it, the end of the road, of our search. We were converted. As I used to say, 'You know when you know that you know.' We were sealed with the Holy

Spirit in the early hours of that morning in September 1972."

When the band arrived Joe rehearsed with them and studied the Bible on the side. He read a verse that said everyone should remain in the situation he was in when God called him. So Joe toured with the band for three more years. But by 1975 the temptations on the road had gotten the better of Joe's faith and he realized after continual backsliding with drugs and women that was not the place for him and left.

CHRISTIAN CULTS AND FALSE TEACHINGS

Joe's zeal for Christianity, plus his guilt over backsliding with the band, opened him up to being spiritually seduced. Joe was soon hooked up with one of many unbalanced Christian cults that have sprung up in our time. A girl on the West Coast wrote him about the extra-anointed brand of Christianity she had found. With its extreme demands on its disciples, she asked, how could it be anything but real?

For a while the Children of God claimed to be the only true Christians. Ditto for the Vine House, or the Apostolic Seven, the Jim Jones sect, The Way International, and so on. These groups rarely converted anyone, but honed in on people converted through other ministries, stealing them away. This is a perfect illustration of the parable of the sower in which the devil's agents try to steal away the new believers. To groups such as these their new revelations, abstinences, and sacrificial lifestyle prove to them that they are the only true Christians on earth.

The girl who wrote Joe was a member of Jim Durkin's Lighthouse Ranch. In the end Joe spent four years on the

West Coast, mostly in Southern California, in Jim Durkin's Shepherding movement. Durkin is a self-appointed apostle. Those in the group come to a point where they passively accept any guidance they are given until they can barely make the simplest decisions for themselves. Joe lived in communal houses, worked, and gave all his earnings to the ministry. Like many cultish groups, they worked to the point of exhaustion, ate poorly, and slept poorly in a communal setting. They were under constant submission to elders, whether they traveled and played music for the community or worked at jobs.

When Joe was at the San Diego commune of Gospel Outreach in 1976 and 1977, he attended Mike MacIntosh's rapidly growing Calvary Chapel Horizon Fellowship and kept wondering why their own small fellowship of thirty never grew beyond that number. When Joe attended Horizon, he was invariably nourished by the teaching and the joy of the fellowship. But it still took several years for Joe to understand.

Joe had to ask permission from the elders to marry Cathy. The elders had chosen another man for her to marry, but finally gave him permission. Joe and Cathy spent two more years with the cult in Oregon, Seattle, and San Diego. They became depleted spiritually. Not only was there no joy for them spiritually but Cathy kept getting sick. She began to battle several skin cancers and other diseases. Meanwhile, after all of their sacrifices for this group, they were given no encouragement or help for Cathy. Joe became bitter. They moved in with Cathy's parents in Whittier, California, in 1979. Joe felt like a failure.

RESTORATION AND MINISTRY

By the time Joe and Cathy left Jim Durkin's cult, Joe's burnout, exhaustion, cynicism, and disillusionment had taken a terrible toll on his soul. Something had been robbed from them. He needed a time of healing as much as he did when he left the band. Joe and Cathy started attending various Calvary Chapels. They left Cathy's parents' house for six months and went to San Diego where they continued going to Horizon Fellowship. God told Joe during this period, after all his exhaustion from striving spiritually and wanting to be in the ministry: *I don't want you in the ministry. I want the ministry to be in you.*

By 1980 they moved back to Whittier and on Thursday nights came to hear me teach at Costa Mesa. Joe felt led to go back to the East Coast. I called him into my office and prayed for him, sensing that good things lay ahead for him in the ministry. They moved to Philadelphia in 1981. By November of that year Joe had found a place to begin a Bible study in Northeast Philadelphia, a catering hall. After six months a hundred people were attending.

In November 1984 Calvary Chapel of Philadelphia moved to their present location, a facility that was formerly a gymnasium. They have four services on Sundays in which 1,000 adults attend. Joe is also on the radio five days a week. Like Bil Gallatin, Joe never asks for money and he never has advertised his ministry. In fact Joe and Bil have never asked for a salary. The elders had to press it upon them. Joe was once told by a skeptical local man, "That's why I trust you. You are not out for money like so many others."

Joe comments that it has been slow going on the East Coast. But once you convert someone you reach into his community. Unlike the West Coast, there are 200-year-old Italian and German neighborhoods in Philadelphia. These people are street smart and, frankly, wary of most things coming out of California. So it is a slow and tough task to prove that you are genuine. Joe's situation is different from, say, that of Jon Courson's in Oregon. It is interesting to see that no one formula works, but that different fellowships seem to find innovative approaches as God directs.

Joe Focht and Bil Gallatin organize joint seasonal trips to Israel for members of their churches. Bil and Joe minister and teach on tour while they refresh one another's ministerial vision. They first became friends when they were roommates during my 1981 tour to Israel for Calvary Chapel pastors. They shared their backgrounds together, laughing and exulting over what God has done in their lives. Meanwhile, at a fellowship for pastors' wives in California, both their wives were randomly assigned as roommates and soon became close friends.

The stories of Bil and Joe plainly illustrate that when God moves in our lives, without our hindrance, doubt, resistance, or manipulation, it is astounding to see what He finally achieves. It is always greater than any of our own ambitions or visions for what is possible in our lives.

Many times people look at Calvary Chapel as something that might work in California, where almost anything goes, but wonder if it would work in the East, where things are supposedly different. They wonder if the God-given principles that work in California would be successful in other parts of the country. Well, we have observed that wherever these principles have been applied, God has blessed. Though people may be different as far as cultural backgrounds go, there is no difference in their common thirst for the truth and for God. At Calvary Chapel these young men have been learning how to bring the Living Water to a thirsty world. And they have seen the same results—nationwide.

11

Mike MacIntosh: Electric Kool-Aid Turns to Everlasting Water

"I thought part of my head missing. When I looked into the mirror, I saw half my face obliterated at times." Beads of sweat gathered on the speaker's forehead as the stage lights in the plush hotel in Hawaii burned down on him.

"For two years I walked around believing that when that forty-five pistol went off only inches from my head, my brains were blown out. I figured it was only by some bizarre fluke of nature that I was able to exist like that. It was terrifying. And there was not a thing in the world I could do about it. I lived in a gray shadow-world—I felt neither dead nor alive. I appeared to be stuck in a plane of consciousness that the world of modern science had not fully accounted for."

It was evident to the audience that this tanned and healthy-looking speaker who stood before them, in his late thirties and radiating exuberant good cheer, was not only "in his right mind and fully clothed," but was now a role model of success for just about any one of them there in that audience of three thousand.

163

The speaker was Mike MacIntosh, and he was recounting the story of his pilgrimage out of an abyss. He had wandered through a certain kind of hell relegated to a small number of drug-trippers in the '60s—the ones who crashed on Owsley Blue Cheers and Yellows and who never fully came back after the trip ended. At the end of his wild, reckless dive into chaos, Mike MacIntosh ended up as a patient in the Crisis Center of Orange County Medical Center. For two years he was under treatment as an outpatient. The prospect for any kind of life at all after that was almost nil.

The '60s generation showed us that America had not yet run out of new frontiers. In the '50s the only things that seemed to dazzle with adventure were 'way out of reach: Space colonization was still in the future and historians pointed backward to illustrate the last of America's new frontiers—valleys of virgin forest, crystal-clear streams and lakes never seen before by civilized men stretching out before them, rippling in nature's silences.

It was easy to romanticize this distant past. Life was inhaled in a gigantic breath; the joys were vivid and the disasters were vivid. Everything was new. By comparison, going to the bowling alley on Friday nights in the mid-1950s seemed dull and pedestrian.

The romance and adventure that come from being on the historical edge, for Americans in the '50s, could only be found in books or the local movie house. America was so stable and its boundaries so fully explored that it grew restless.

When the '60s arrived that restlessness sprang into action. Bob Dylan, Frank Zappa, and others started telling the older generation that they were trivial people from a trivial world doomed to extinction in the coming revolution, a revolution of consciousness, an anarchy of belief and morals. Indeed a new frontier had been discovered—mind-altering drugs. Soon the social revolution of the '60s would change the face of America. Newness and adventure were back on the horizon, but at a price like never before.

It is interesting to walk through Berkeley's People's Park in 1987, twenty years after the psychedelic revolution. The old gurus have quieted. Instead there are now the squatter groups in the park, the mutterers and twitchers who had been the youth of the '60s and who are now street people. The new yuppie generation at Cal Berkeley is career-oriented. They look with disdain at these has-beens—the pioneers of LSD who burned the flag and dropped out. The yuppies have shelved the quest for higher truth and are working instead to get their careers established. And if they do get "high" now it is strictly for pleasure: cocaine, and not psychedelics, is the preferred drug for them.

Not only has the hippies' heyday passed, but the excesses of the past have caught up with them. Many are now welfare cases, cared for by the very system they tried to destroy. They are unable to contribute to society or even pay their own way. When they were at the pinnacle of youthful energy, tanned, smiling, and getting high in the California sun, I bet that if they had been shown a movie of how they would turn out they would have screamed in horror, thrown their pills and reefers into the Pacific, and questioned their own dreams.

Some of them did this, of course. They saw something down below, a glimpse of hell, if you will, that made them stop in their tracks. Mike MacIntosh was one of them, escaping this inferno by the skin of his teeth.

His narration in the auditorium in Maui, as always, could not escape that occasional dip into the bizarre, the absurd, of the comic lampooning himself.

First of all there were the "pre-launch" descriptions. "I was in the Yucca Valley at four in the morning on LSD chanting my TM mantra. Below was a white-domed building. Some pals told me that it was a space machine that gave off electromagnetic pulses, and would take me back in time. Around the side of the hill nearby was a small airport. A UFO was due to arrive anytime." He had been lured there by a local cult figure named Ron who was a drug-pusher and considered himself the new messiah. Ron was into Zen, yoga, and Satan worship.

Little wonder Mike wanted to board a UFO. His outer world at that time, 1969, had little to be desired. At twenty-four years of age his marriage was beyond salvaging. His wife had fled with the kids. A spaceman for a father was not what she had in mind. He was thousands of dollars in debt to people he had cunningly hustled. He was about to be fired from work. Mike MacIntosh had taken frequent doses of LSD and other drugs and his thinking was getting more and more skewed. He was ripe for a California saucer cult headed by a deceptive leader like Ron, whose one-story, brown-shingled shack, was perched on the edge of a canyon. One thing could be said, Ron was never boring or predictable. Like many psychopaths, he had no sense of responsibility for what became of those who put their souls at his disposal. The vulnerable, naïve, or credulous are textbook victims in the hands of people like Ron.

Describing his own descent into the abyss, Mike must have run a chord of familiarity with many in that auditorium in Hawaii.

"One night I was left off at Ron's by a pal who had given me a gift—LSD laced with rat poison, strychnine. My speech and vision were blurring rapidly and I was getting more and more paranoid every second. Everything became evidence of a conspiracy. Unfortunately there was plenty of evidence around. Ron looked like he was on the floor loading forty-five caliber shells into his pistol, surrounded by gaping followers. I suddenly suspected that Ron was a Mafia hit man hired to get me by my secret enemies."

Fear, when detected by some people, becomes a growing source of power. This is an evil dynamic seen in certain occult groups. Ron picked up on Mike's terror and played on it. A sadistic game ensued.

"I thrashed around yelling, 'Ron, help, I've OD'd.' "

Ron shoved another bullet into the chamber of the revolver. "You're okay," he responded in a disgusted tone. "No problem."

Mike continued, "At a sign from Ron, I thought I felt those in the room grabbing me. They took off my shoes, socks, and my shirt. Tied my hands behind my back. Then they tied a cloth bag over my head. I knew I was going to die and I started screaming. I saw spirit forms floating by and I called out to them wondering if they were God or knew God. Among them was Maharishi who had promised that for one hundred and thirty-four dollars he could take me to God."

The degradation rose to new levels. "I squirmed into a bedroom. Then I pressed my forehead against the floor to pray. Then I felt the barrel of the revolver pressed against my head. Suddenly I heard a deafening explosion. A forty-five pistol exploding only inches from your head is devastating. Try that amplified by the power of LSD. My head was gone, I knew it. My brains had been blown out. In truth it was either a blank or they fired at the wall, but to me on LSD that was it. The problem was that this perception of my brains being blown out stayed with me for over two years."

A week after the incident Mike, obviously giving out "help" signals, handed himself over to the Laguna Beach police, telling them that he was with the Beatles. He had been nurturing this delusion for over a year.

"That afternoon, spirit voices directed me to baptize myself in the Pacific, then go down Pacific Coast Highway handing out my LP rock records. My words to the police receptionist were: 'Ma'am, I'm with the Beatles, and they're in town doing a nude pop art reproduction of the resurrection of Jesus Christ in a yellow submarine.' "

This usually gets chuckles from an audience, and did that day in Hawaii. But like the two masks of Greek theater, there is an infinitely sad expression behind the grin of the comic. Insanity is a kind of hell. It is lonely, it is terrifying. In many ways, it is the final alienation from all things. First people, then finally reality itself.

Shirwood Wirt, author of *For the Love of Mike*, describes this touching, pathetic moment after Mike's words to the police:

"It was a beautiful February day in southern California. Mockingbirds were singing and the blossoms were on the peach trees, but for Michael MacIntosh life had lost its beauty. He knew he had touched bottom. The easy charm, the puckish, fun-loving demeanor had failed him. Not often had Michael been reduced to tears—once when his older brother, David, was slammed into a telephone pole and killed; once when he broke up with a high school sweetheart; and once, most agonizingly, when Sandra moved out with little Melinda. But on this Sunday morning, Michael cried because he was in a holding tank, locked in the mental ward of a hospital with some strange-looking characters; and he was not getting out."

Now, as he relayed this story before his audience, this former patient was the pastor of perhaps the largest church in San Diego, Horizon Christian Fellowship. It had grown to 5,000, and Mike was a popular speaker. He was also soon to appear on national television, giving his testimony at the huge Billy Graham Crusade in Anaheim. Not bad for a broke and psychotic street hippie trapped in an Orange County holding tank. It was a historical fact, Mike had not only been transformed by Christ, but he now lived an enviably productive life.

And, frankly, I never cease to be amazed at this miracle myself. I well remember the night at Calvary Chapel Costa Mesa that Mike stood up, and finally came forward to dedicate his life to Christ. In those days, in April of 1970, he certainly blended in with the sea of youth at our church in bare feet and long hair whom we always welcomed, just as they were. Christ would have done no less.

Yet when Mike and I talked later, I frankly wondered whether he would ever come back down to earth. For during those petulant years of the late '60s and early '70s, we had thousands of youth like Mike who had come to us from the hippie culture. Not everyone made it, so deeply had they fallen in their search for spiritual reality. Many thought they had found it in psychedelics. They felt that their mandate was to create a world of love and peace by getting everyone stoned at the same time, their own version of heaven on earth.

Woodstock was to be a dramatic demonstration to the world of the utopia possible when masses of people become stoned together, drop their "head-games," and just "groove" on rock music. True, a few had fun. But there remained the reality of drug overdoses, orgies, rapes, fights, and stealing, to sully the anticipated picture of perfect harmony and brotherly love. And the food system barely held for the three days. By the time the half-million horde left "Woodstock Nation" in Upstate New York, the once verdant fields were flattened, and tons of trash blew in the wind. Rain had created a massive field of sludge, which they had danced in as the rock festival wore into its third day. Perhaps the sludge was a metaphor for what was to come.

Within a matter of months, the second utopian experiment was under way. The Rolling Stones had a massive concert at Altamont, California. But this event became a horrible nightmare for the thousands. Pandemonium set in. There was even more violence, rapes, and beatings. And this time there were killings. The Hell's Angels, serving as "police," had stabbed a man, and that triggered the chaos. It happened while Mick Jagger was singing "Sympathy for the Devil." The Hell's Angels stormed to the front to kill the first troublemaker and make an example of him to the rather wimpy flower people who were shoving toward the stage. When the fellow produced a switchblade, that was all it took for the Angels to crush him. By the end of Altamont concert, the hippie utopian dream of universal brotherhood and love was shattered. They had touted the Rousseau ideal of the innocent or noble savage: that unfettered by civilization, man was basically good and innocent. But what people saw in themselves and others while on drugs was a magnitude of sheer perversity, cruelty, hardness, and selfishness that was terrifying. This reality signaled the end of the hippie era.

After Altamont, disillusioned and broken, many of the victims of the drug culture showed up on our steps at Calvary Chapel. We heard some incredible stories. Many of these kids had so fried their minds with various powerful substances that they would never recover from the damage. They had gone too far into a world of fantasy and could not find their way back to reality. Some of them injected almost anything into their veins, including peanut butter, in search of a new kind of "high."

So for the first six months, as Mike MacIntosh would share his fantasy world, we wondered if he was one of the permanent casualties. But gradually we saw changes that were encouraging signs to us. We saw God begin to restore the years that the canker worm had eaten.

Within months of his conversion, we moved twenty-six-year-old Mike, who had been floating from house to house, or living in a shack at Newport Beach, into a house that we established. Its real ministry was to offer newly converted youth, who had been rootless, a place that they could call home. God showed us a tangible need and we responded as best as we could.

Youth who had been bound by drugs gained freedom in Jesus. They washed and worked together in an environment of love—true love, Christ's love. They worked hard and grew in character as they faced the responsibility of sticking to decisions. This meant moral restraint and self-control. If they had squandered years in reckless abandon, old habits had to be overcome. But the smile of innocence did return. And the changing condition of our home for them reflected their own inner changes. Many scraped, painted, and rebuilt the house. Others went out and got responsible jobs and put money back into the house. They paid their debts and learned to face the responsibilities of adulthood.

Clearly God was the power behind this radical change. The house community prayed, extended themselves unselfishly to others, and studied their Redeemer within the pages of the Bible. This was anything but cheap escapism for youth who had grown accustomed to the easy life of hedonism, when they could do what they wanted anytime. Meanwhile, Mike MacIntosh grew like a fern in a greenhouse. He was becoming a gifted leader and teacher, as he assumed more and more responsibilities over the house ministry.

But there were still tangible reminders of Mike's failed past. Sandy, Mike's ex-wife, was back in town. Before, when he had first met her, he charmed her with every image and facade he could, inventing one incredible story after another. He, a high school dropout, read passages from high-sounding books to seem knowledgeable to this college coed. He claimed to be a med student from the University of Oregon. Other times the story was different.

After only several weeks of knowing Mike, Sandy agreed to drive to Las Vegas, on a spree, and marry him. It was a twelve-dollar civil ceremony. And they took their vows in blue jeans and bare feet. Soon enough Mike's glitter tarnished. Sandy finally saw the utter contradiction of his life. By then this pretty and devoted girl had been forced to drop out of college to support them and their little girl while he surfed and got stoned. It was too much. So, pregnant for the second time, she fled back to the luxurious home of her affluent parents back East. Their contempt for this social outcast had been proven right.

Of course, if you know the whole story of Mike MacIntosh, when he was a boy growing up in Oregon, then there is another side to consider. We see a sad tale of a youth with promise being shattered by the sledgehammer of circumstance. There was a time, in his sunnier, more innocent years, when Mike made straight A's and was a star baseball player. He excelled in the Cub Scouts, had lots of friends, and by early high school, he was voted student of the year. Mike, in those days, was willing to trust all and everyone. He had the cherubic smile of a sunrise. Sensitivity and vulnerability were in his nature. And even though life had always been tough for Mike, he had always been able to rise above it, looking on the bright side. He kept this up through the hungry and uncertain years of a repeatedly broken home and the poverty that accompanied it.

But eventually the world beat Mike down. His allotment of misfortune seemed 'way out of proportion to that of other people. Everything that ever meant anything to him was taken away bit by bit till he felt he had nothing.

First of all, there was the distant alcoholic father he never knew. When he finally did get the father-figure he had yearned for, the third man his mother had married, suddenly even this was taken away. The stepfather left. This was a blow. But the final blow for Mike came when his older brother, a model and hero figure, was killed in a car accident. Suddenly, life had the bitter taste of a cosmic joke. And if life is a joke, then you treat it like a joke. Mike dropped out of high school, joined the Army for a while, then went on his solitary pilgrimage down the road. By the time he met Sandy, he was a seasoned beach bum who knew how to manipulate and hustle people to get what he wanted. He saw no hope for the future so he learned to live for the brief pleasures of the moment.

Now Sandy was back trying to finish college, this time without Mike to spoil her life.

But Mike still had the legal right as father to see his child. And now that he was a Christian, it was hard for Sandy not to notice the change in him. But it seemed too good to be true, Sandy reminded herself. Besides, Mike had cried wolf too many times. Sandy watched Mike with a critical eye. But she kept seeing that this change in him was real; it had substance. Finally, without his manipulating her, she went to a Calvary Chapel beach concert, during the time he was living in the community home, and that did it. Sandy could not deny the same spirit of love, in Christians who packed the beach, that she had seen in Mike. When an invitation to accept Christ was given, Sandy, in tears, knelt to give her life to Christ. I have no doubt that God knew that Mike needed Sandy, for his life and for his ministry.

The day I had the privilege of remarrying Mike and Sandy, with little blonde Mindy serving as flower girl, the tears of joy flowed freely for we knew that God's restoration was complete. In fact the wedding had to be stopped right in the middle because so many people were sobbing so hard, including the bride and the groom. That touching moment is hard to describe.

As Mike developed during the house community era and beyond, it was obvious that he had leadership ability and was an excellent communicator. His track record in retail sales showed that he was responsible and hardworking. He was also very interested in music, so when we started "Maranatha! Music" with our first album, a demo featuring all of our groups, Mike became our first distributor. In those days, he would fill the trunk of his car with albums and travel throughout California entreating the Christian bookstores to stock this new kind of Christian music. It worked and sales started to take off. As Mike proved his abilities, we turned Maranatha! Music over to him, and he became the director. But Mike's first love remained his desire to communicate his faith to audiences in an evangelistic context. The music ran a close second only because he could see that it captured the attention of the audience and could create an opening for more direct communication.

As director of Maranatha! Music Mike was also in the role of road manager of the various bands. Thus, when they were on tour, he used the break time between sets to come out and give his testimony or share some burden on his heart. These fleeting appearances on stage began to be those prime-time moments that Mike longed for. He knew by the eyes of the audience that he was getting through to them. By the time he traveled with a band and various musicians to Manila to play before 15,000 a night, Mike was getting impressive results as a communicator during these break periods between sets.

About this time in 1975 some students came to me from San Diego State, asking if I could send someone to San Diego to start a church. They had been driving up each week for the services at Calvary Chapel. Immediately I thought of Mike, knowing that he was God's choice for this task. Mike had already been commuting weekly to San Diego to teach at their rapidly expanding Bible study at the Hospitality House at Balboa Park.

Yet when I told Mike that I was going to give him a month's vacation with pay, and that during that month he was to move to San Diego to start a Calvary Chapel, he was devastated. He had come to look upon me as the father he had never had and it was, for him, like a father telling his son to leave home. But because he loved me as a dad he moved to San Diego without hesitation to work as hard as possible to make me proud of my son in the faith.

In just a few months' time Mike invited me down to speak before his Wednesday night Bible study, which by then was meeting in a large church auditorium in Linda Vista. And indeed I could not have been more proud and thrilled as I saw the hundreds of shining young faces jamming that auditorium beyond its capacity, who were now among the countless converts to Jesus Christ due to Mike's ministry. Sunday services in that auditorium were running well over a thousand.

In less than a year Mike consulted us about purchasing the North Park Theater, where Burns & Allen and Sophie Tucker once played. This grand theater was needed to seat the thousands of young people who were showing up. We helped them purchase the theater, which was soon beautifully refurbished. On Sundays the marquee had crowds streaming out onto University Avenue, through three packed services, while the massive stage glittered with musicians with drums and electric guitars, acoustic guitars, horns, and all manner of keyboards surrounded by loudspeakers that were taller than the musicians.

At North Park the music was electric. And when Mike came out to speak you could hear a pin drop. Rolled up in this communicator was a virtuoso of humor, irony, pointed insight, and endless stories. He was spontaneous as he *ad libbed* or mimed or became the comic, making fun of himself. Beneath it all was a vibrant awareness of God's grace and love, all of which he brought to bear on Scripture. And no one could seem to get enough of it.

Here was one of them who had been touched by God and they marveled over this. It gave them hope, the surfers, trippers, and yuppies. There was almost no trip they had done that Mike hadn't done. And when he spoke it was with the authority of someone who knew what he was talking about and believed deeply. Sometimes he was in a colorful tee shirt, other times he wore a coat and tie, but beneath it all was a deadly serious concern for the souls before him.

Mike then started a school for evangelism and began to train hundreds of young people to share their faith. He also began to give birth to other churches in San Diego County as he encouraged key people in leadership to spread out from the home church and start their own. If you ask Mike he will probably tell you that he is more of an evangelist than a Bible expositor. He might even tell you that he has a secret yearning to be on the road speaking at rallies, even more than staying put with the responsibility of a church. So far he has been able to do both.

I pray that Mike always remains open to the Spirit, never forgets who he was and is, and keeps on learning humbly. I also pray that he never becomes disqualified through pride or any other pitfall. All of us in the ministry must constantly be under the admonition, "He who thinks he stands, let him take heed, lest he fall." Like all of us, Mike has scars from the past and weaknesses that, if not surrendered to the Holy Spirit, could get the better of him. Our refuge should be never to forget our first love. Nor should we forget the spiritual desert experiences of our past, when things were not so easy. As easy as it was for God to bring us into a season of blessings, I always keep in mind that He could just as easily put us back on the shelf again. May God ever get the glory!

Today every major community in San Diego County has a Horizon/Calvary Chapel, and the home church, Horizon Christian Fellowship, has moved to an enormous school complex that houses an auditorium, a cafeteria, tennis courts, basketball courts, a gym, classrooms, a bookstore. Mike is on radio and TV shows, his church publishes a widely distributed magazine called *Horizon International Magazine,* and the numerous evangelistic missions of his school of evangelism to various foreign countries have had far-reaching effects.

Of all the Calvary Chapel affiliate pastors, I think that the life of Mike MacIntosh shows the greatest healing and deliverance from the widest range of cultural depravities to beset this '60s generation of Calvary Chapel pastors. Mike had been stained with such depravities as madness, drugs, shattered ethics and morals, as well as divorce in his parents' marriage and his own marriage. I have seen Mike MacIntosh change from a hopeless beach bum, mental case, and divorcé, to a man who is sane, dedicated, and devout. He is now a responsible husband and father, whose far-reaching ministry has become a phenomenon. If that does not show that God is real, and satisfy the skeptic, I am not sure what does!

Let us now prayerfully seek the help of the Holy Spirit to understand the simple biblical principles that Mike and these other men learned at Calvary Chapel, things that I had to learn through years of experience in struggle and failure. Are these truths transferable? Can others, even without formal Bible training, follow these principles and develop large and effective ministries? Hundreds of strong churches seem to say yes.

12

Principles to Grow By

Many churches are built around the personality of the pastor and as a result the work cannot be duplicated and the concepts are not transferable. Trying to imitate another person's personality is never successful. God has made us all unique individuals and His Spirit anoints us according to our own individual characteristics.

Many times a pastor who is anxious to see church growth makes the mistake of going to large, successful churches, looking at their programs, and watching the way the minister relates to his people. Then the pastor tries to copy the program and the personality. And it just doesn't work.

It is true that God does work through personalities; they play a very important part in the way we relate to people. But because Calvary Chapel has been built on principles rather than personalities, the principles are transferable and work in all varieties of personalities. Through following these simple steps Calvary Chapel pastors have found tremendously successful ministries. Let me share them with you.

When I first began in the ministry I served in a denomination whose main emphasis was evangelism. This was

179

reflected by the fact that the first bit of information required on my monthly report was the number of people saved. The next box was for the number of people baptized. I had heard so often that the primary purpose of the Church was the evangelization of the world, thus every sermon that I preached was somehow brought around to evangelism and the appeal made for people to accept Jesus Christ as their Lord and Savior.

My greatest frustration would come when I would prepare what I felt to be a powerful evangelistic sermon that would surely convert the most hardened sinner. And when I would arrive at church to my dismay there was not a single sinner in the whole congregation.

As I would sit on the platform looking over the congregation—I knew them all by first name—I knew there wasn't a sinner in the house. During the song service I'd pray that God would somehow send sinners in and when my prayers were not answered I had to preach my evangelistic sermon to the saints with no hope of conversions. As a general rule I would add a few points in which I would castigate those in the congregation for their failures to be the kind of witnesses that the Lord wanted them to be. Surely, I told them, if they were serving the Lord and were doing what God wanted them to do they would have brought some of their neighbors along to hear the Word of God and to be saved. I would begin to beat the sheep because they were not effectively reproducing or witnessing for Jesus Christ.

My heart aches when I think of those early days of my ministry, how I was creating guilt-ridden, frustrated believers. They were guilt-ridden because what I was saying was correct: They weren't being the kind of witness that they should be for Christ. Their lives weren't measuring up to biblical standards. They were frustrated because they desired to live victorious lives and be witnesses but they just didn't know how because their pastor was emphasizing evangelism rather than feeding the Body of Christ.

This was the first lesson. Traditionally I felt that the primary purpose of the Church was the evangelization of the world. But biblically, Paul in Ephesians 4 tells us that the primary purpose of the Church is to build up the Body of Christ to perfect the saints for the work of the ministry. To bring them into a maturity and a unity of the faith so that they would no longer be as babes but might fully develop in Christ Jesus. With my constant emphasis on the repentance from dead works and the doctrines of baptism, I had failed to bring the people into a fully matured relationship with the Lord and they stayed in a state of spiritual infancy.

The second lesson in my own ministry came in an interesting way.

My messages were topical, taken from Scriptures throughout the Bible. There was no consistent pattern in my preaching. One week my text might be from Matthew, the next week from Isaiah, the following week from Revelation, and the following from Genesis. I would share whatever topic happened to interest me that week or whatever Scripture might have just spoken to me. The most difficult part of the ministry at that time was finding a text from which to preach. I would find myself reading a book of the Bible until some Scripture sort of stood out in my mind and then I would develop from that text my message. I found that I had about two years of good topical sermons before I ran out of ideas and so my first few pastorates were of two years' duration. After I had exhausted my two years' of texts, I would seek a transfer to another church. This continued until we lived in Huntington Beach. We were coming close to the end of our two years and it was time to move again, but a problem had developed: We had fallen in love with Huntington Beach! We enjoyed living there and our little girl had now started school. We did not want to leave.

Suddenly I was under pressure to find more texts and more sermons. About this time I was reading the book *The Apostle John* by Griffith Thomas. In one of the chapters he had outlined studies on 1 John. As I studied those outlines I found that they were excellent sermon material and there were approximately forty of them. I decided that if I taught through the book of 1 John on Sunday mornings, we could spend another year in this community that we had come to love. I bought several commentaries on 1 John and began an exhaustive study of the epistle. I expanded the outline studies of Griffith Thomas and we spent a year on 1 John.

The interesting thing is that during this year our church experienced greater growth than we had ever seen before. We also had more conversions and more baptisms than we had ever experienced in the past. The people were suddenly filled with joy in their walk with Christ, they were experiencing greater power over sin, and they had a greater assurance of their salvation. Of course, these are the three reasons why John wrote the epistle and we are told that God's Word will not return void but will accomplish the purposes for which it was sent. Inasmuch as this epistle was sent to bring the believers into the fullness of joy, freedom from sin, and assurance of their salvation, God's Word did its work within their lives.

And I learned the second lesson: Expositional teaching is stronger than topical teaching for feeding the flock.

At the end of the year we still did not want to leave Huntington Beach. Having developed, now, the style of teaching straight through a book, I decided to take the book of Romans next, which a seminary professor had told us would transform any church. I bought as many commentaries as I could find on the book of Romans, and spent two years teaching on it. During this time the church doubled. The work of the Spirit in the hearts of the people was electrifying as they discovered, and as I personally discovered, the grace of God and began to relate to God in a new way. It was about this time that I purchased a new Halley's *Bible Handbook.* (I was always giving mine away to the new converts.)

On the flyleaf I saw a notation that said the most important page in the book was page 814. So I turned to that page to find out what Mr. Halley felt was the most important thing. There was the simple suggestion that every church have a congregational plan of Bible reading, and that the pastor's sermon be from the part of the Bible read the past week. I had never taken the people through the whole Bible. As a matter of fact I had never sat down to read the Bible straight through.

So I incorporated the third lesson: I decided that I would start the congregation reading the whole Bible, ten chapters a week, and that my sermon would come out of the chapters that they had read. I have been following this practice now for many years and have seen people in the church, for the first time in their lives, read the Bible all the way through.

These two transitions—from topical messages to expository teaching to working straight through the Bible—

have taught me some very fascinating things. Number one, I came to the realization that during the years of my topical ministry I did not have a true Bible emphasis in my preaching. Though I preached every sermon from the Scriptures, my preaching was not biblically balanced. The Scriptures tell of God's part and of man's part. The majority of the topical sermons that I preached were emphasizing man's part. Sermons exhorting the people to pray, to witness, to commitment, exhorting the people to serve.

But when you get into a book of the Bible and continue straight through, you find there is a greater emphasis on what God has done for man than what man should be doing for God. In a sense, through the topical sermons, I was emphasizing what we should be doing for God in order that God might respond to us. I was making man the initiator and God the respondent. For instance, if you give, God will give back to you, measured out, pressed down, running over. If you praise, you will be blessed with a sense of His presence, for He inhabits the praises of His people. If you will win souls, you will be wise and shine as the stars forever.

But now I learned that God was the initiator so His part is always first. Take the book of Ephesians as an example. Paul spends the first three chapters of Ephesians telling the church what God had done for them. He prefaces this section with these words: "Blessed be the God and Father of our Lord Jesus Christ, who has blessed us with every spiritual blessing in the heavenly places in Christ ." And then he lists the glorious spiritual blessings and benefits that we have from God. It is not until he gets to chapter four that he deals with human responsibility by exhorting them to walk worthy of this calling wherewith they were called.

God was the initiator and now Paul exhorted man to respond to God. I found that when people began to discover who God is and all that God has done, they were eager to respond to God and did not have to be pushed or exhorted to pray or to serve. Now they were volunteering their service, their time—they could not do enough for the Lord as they came to the recognition of what He had done for them.

The second thing I learned from these lessons was that evangelism is the natural byproduct of a healthy church. When, in the early years of my ministry, I had placed an emphasis constantly on their going out and winning someone to Jesus Christ, the numbers of people that were coming to the Lord were very small. When I began to feed the Body of Christ with the Word of God, we had more conversions and baptisms in the first year than we had had in any previous year of our ministry. And as the people continued to grow, the numbers the next year were doubled and it just continued to go that way because the people now were strong and they were healthy.

Then we happened on the third interesting change to come out of these experiences. Christmas and Easter Sundays were bedlam. There were always so many people coming to Sunday school and to church that the facilities couldn't hold them. Thus, those who would come only once or twice a year would come during the most trying circumstances, which didn't really encourage them to come back on a regular basis.

To deal with the problem of overcrowded rooms and the confusion in general, we decided that on Christmas and Easter we would not have Sunday school followed by church, but would have Sunday school for the children and Sunday morning service for the adults simultaneously. We had found in the past that many people would come to Sunday school and leave before church and thus never hear the Gospel. So by bringing the adults together for teaching they had greater opportunity to receive the Gospel message.

Everyone loved it so much we continued the practice year-round. We also discovered that with the children being taught on their own grade levels and not being present in the sanctuary during the service that the attention level of the adults was much higher. They were able to understand and absorb much more without the distractions of their children around them. In this new arrangement, having the morning service and Sunday school running concurrently, I became, in a sense, the teacher of the adult class that happened to be held in the main sanctuary. Later on we slipped naturally into the fourth lesson: double services. This worked out even better because then those who were teaching Sunday school could attend the next service, and it provided us with a lot more volunteers for the Sunday school program.

In going to double services we found that a smaller auditorium and smaller facilities were able to accommodate twice the number of people. So when we were in our building program we deliberately built the auditorium and facility with the intention of having double services. We found that there were those who loved coming earlier, there were those who loved coming later, and we were able to enlarge the total membership without enlarging the facilities or the staff. As an added benefit we now had two congregations supporting one facility. This meant that one of the congregations could support our local program and the surplus funds could be diverted into mission ventures. When we were later built to triple services, it was even more exciting, for we were able then to give two-thirds of our budget to missions while using only one-third of the total funds for our own local needs. This pattern continues to the present day.

And, then, I learned the fifth lesson for building a strong church. We were experiencing such growth and so many new converts that we soon caught the attention of our superiors. When a large church in our district had an opening, I was asked to take it. While in that church, a group became interested in the work of the Holy Spirit. They invited me to come and begin a Bible study in their homes, for they declared that they knew very little of the Bible apart from the readings in their prayer book. That Bible study soon grew so large that we had to break it into two.

The importance of having home Bible studies was an invaluable lesson. In these home Bible studies I developed a whole new style of teaching. Rather than the Sunday oratory style, I would just sit and talk in a very natural way. They would feel the freedom to interrupt when they did not understand a particular passage or interpretation of the passage, and it would turn into animated discussions. I found that their attention span was increased. In church after thirty minutes of preaching people were restless. But we could sit for an hour-and-a-half to two hours in the home and then the people would actually be disappointed that I stopped.

Later on when we started Calvary Chapel, we started several home Bible studies. The one on Monday night was geared for the young people and I would more or less "rap" with them as we sat in the living room of a home in

Costa Mesa. The group soon became so large that we no longer fit in the home. Kids were sitting in the dining room, kitchen, up the stairway, in the entry hall, and there would be more outside who couldn't get in. We were, at that time, building our first chapel. The slab had been poured, so at night we would set up lights and the kids would sit on the slab and I would sit there with them. We just built the chapel walls up around them as time went on. It was during this time that we began to reach hundreds of the young people who had been involved in the hippie culture. They loved the informality of sitting outside and having the teacher just sit there and talk with them rather than preach at them.

From these informal talks I developed the style of teaching in a natural, almost conversational way. I just talk with the congregation about the things of God, of the glories of His nature, of His Kingdom. I found that if I'm talking—rather than preaching—the attention span holds for an hour as they sit with open Bibles learning God's Word. A half-hour of preaching can wear people out, but an hour of teaching, if it's done in an easy conversational way, does not.

These are not complicated lessons. In fact, the secret that I seek to impart to those eager to enter the ministry is to simply teach the Word of God simply. Tradition can be a hard thing to overcome, but lack of church growth can be more discouraging. It's been exciting to watch Calvary Chapels all across the country grow as the power of God touches people's lives. The harvest of souls into the Kingdom of God is our goal. May God ever receive the glory and honor due His name.

Another important principle that pastors learn at Calvary Chapel is complete dependence on the Holy Spirit to help them in expounding the Word. Jesus said that the Holy Spirit would teach them all things and bring to their remembrance the things that they had been taught. Paul said that the natural man could not understand the things of the Spirit neither could he know them for they were spiritually discerned. What is found at Calvary Chapel is the Spirit of God working through the Word of God to change the people of God.

There are many churches that offer excellent teaching of the Bible, but almost deny the current work of the Spirit of God. This creates dead orthodoxy. The people may be well versed in the Scriptures but it has not altered their lifestyles to any great extent. They have a form of godliness but have denied the power.

On the other side of the coin are churches that emphasize the Holy Spirit but neglect teaching from the Word. This leads to emotionalism and an unstable condition that is open to every wind of doctrine and cunning craftiness of men who are standing by ready to deceive. Many heretical teachers have found fertile soil in church congregations that overemphasize only emotional experiences. It is so important to have a balance of the Word and the Spirit so that you can see the life-changing power of God at work and a stable growth of the Body of Christ.

At Calvary Chapel we have confidence that when God guides, God provides, so there is never an emphasis on money or giving. Many of our churches do not even pass the plate, but place a box at the entrance where the people who desire may contribute. God is never represented as being broke or facing imminent bankruptcy. The pastors have been taught that God is perfectly capable of supplying the needs for the things He desires to see accomplished. God does not need the support of His people to stay in business; the people need the support of God.

It is sad to see people driven away from the church by the appeals and gimmicks that have been used to solicit funds. Some have dropped out of church because they had nothing to give and felt embarrassed. We do not let this happen to them at Calvary because they are never asked to give or to pledge. As the apostle Paul said, never let your giving be by pressure or constraint, but let every man give as he has purposed in his own heart, for God loves a cheerful giver.

If you asked people who visited Calvary Chapel what impressed them the most, you would probably hear a variety of things, but some of the words that you would hear most often would be: warm, loving, worshipful, casual. The first impression as you walk into the service is the warmth of God's love among His people. You see a lot of hugging, which probably goes back to the days of the hippies. There is a lot of happiness and laughter. There is also a reverent but casual atmosphere, which is reflected in the styles of clothes the people wear. They do not feel that they need to get dressed up to attend church. Yet if they are dressed up they do not feel uncomfortable. There is an acceptance of the person not the style of clothing. This again goes back to the hippie days when all kinds of clothes and styles were worn. Chuck Girard who was singing with the Love Song group in the earlier days of Calvary expressed it very well in his song "Little Country Church" with the lines: "Long hair, short hair,/Some coats and ties,/People finally coming around,/ Looking past the hair,/Straight into the eyes."

The music at Calvary Chapel is fresh and alive, and filled with worship choruses. Many times a worship group will lead the singing accompanied by guitars, drums, keyboards. Many of the choruses are composed by the leaders in the worship groups and are passed on to the other Calvary Chapels. This gives quite a contemporary feel. Often a young person will share a song and explain that the Lord just gave him the song that afternoon.

Most of the churches in the U.S. today are highly organized and highly structured. By this I mean they stress the dependence that the church has on the people and the dependence the people have on the church. At Calvary Chapel we prefer a looser structure, as we stress our total dependency on God. It is interesting that most of the people in the U.S. today fit more comfortably into an independent, casual catagory; thus, we fish almost alone in a huge, well-stocked pond, while many other churches try to fish in a much smaller pond.

In the book of Acts we are told that when the Church was born the believers continued steadfastly in the apostles' doctrine, fellowship, breaking of bread, and prayers. These are the four features that marked the early Church; these are the features that mark the Calvary Chapels. These are the things that are emphasized, sought after, and practiced, and we have discovered that—as in the early Church—the Lord adds to our numbers daily.

The result of seeing this work of the Lord with its remarkable fruit is one obvious conclusion: "To God be the glory, great things He has done."